The New York Times

IN THE HEADLINES

Fake News

READ ALL ABOUT IT

THE NEW YORK TIMES EDITORIAL STAFF

Published in 2019 by New York Times Educational Publishing
in association with The Rosen Publishing Group, Inc.
29 East 21st Street, New York, NY 10010

Distributed exclusively by Rosen Publishing.

First Edition

The New York Times
Alex Ward: Editorial Director, Book Development
Brenda Hutchings: Senior Photo Editor / Art Buyer
Phyllis Collazo: Photo Rights / Permissions Editor
Heidi Giovine: Administrative Manager

Rosen Publishing
Jacob R. Steinberg: Director of Content Development
Greg Tucker: Creative Director
Brian Garvey: Art Director
Greg Clinton: Editor

Cataloging-in-Publication Data
Names: New York Times Company.
Title: Fake news: read all about it / edited by the New York Times editorial staff.
Description: New York : The New York Times Educational Publishing, 2019. | Series: In the headlines | Includes glossary and index.
Identifiers: ISBN 9781642820225 (pbk.) | ISBN 9781642820218 (library bound) | ISBN 9781642820201 (ebook)
Subjects: LCSH: Fake news—Juvenile literature. | Journalism—History—21st century—Juvenile literature.
Classification: LCC PN4784.F27 F354 2019 | DDC 070.4'3—dc23

Manufactured in the United States of America

On the cover: Headlines published from New York Times articles.

Contents

CHAPTER 4

Donald Trump and Weaponizing Fake News

CHAPTER 5

Fake News Around the World

Introduction

FAKE NEWS IS NOT one single phenomenon. First and most simply, fake news is a published news report that can be easily proved false. This kind of "fake" means that the story doesn't correspond with reality — as if a neighbor said, "It's raining outside, don't go out!" and you opened the door to reveal a cloudless spring day.

Moreover, fake news is not simply a falsehood; it has broad appeal and is seen by many people. Successful fake news is shocking, exciting, or confirms some belief you hold deeply (so you are less likely to be skeptical of it and more likely to share it with friends.) So if a neighbor tells you it's raining outside, you might be annoyed by the lie, but no one else would be impacted. If, however, your neighbor started a weather news channel and had some reason to convince people that it was raining outside, and published a story that went viral that was all about acid rain that's eating through the pavement outside your home, and millions of people decided to stay inside that day ... now we're closer to what fake news looks like today. It is a deliberate attempt to sway public opinion using false and explosive claims.

"Explosive" is exciting but also dangerous. Fake news can be a weapon. President Donald Trump has used the term as an accusation against any media outlet that writes about him unfavorably. The intended effect is to cast doubt on a damaging or critical story — whether or not the story is true — and to sow skepticism of major news media in general. The logic goes: if people can't trust the news media, they will trust the president himself, armed with direct access to his thoughts via a Twitter feed that only ever expresses "truth".

In other ways, fake news is being weaponized through social media to influence global political contests. Russia has been at the center of

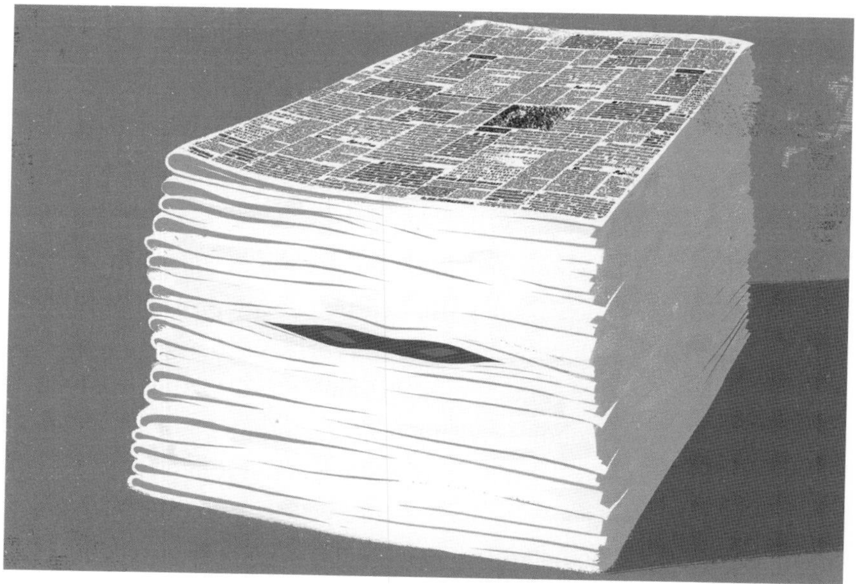

CARLO GIAMBARRESI

recent investigations around the world that accuse President Vladimir Putin's administration and its cyber-warfare allies of using viral fake news stories to inflame political discord in other countries (usually democratic rivals like the United States, Germany, Italy, France, and Great Britain). Their purpose is to sway the outcomes of democratic elections in order to advance Russian economic and political interests.

In effect, fake news is a weapon that is taking aim at the practice of democracy. Undermining truth and public trust in responsible investigative reporting weakens the freedoms that many people around the world want to enjoy. It makes democracy measurably weaker as an effective and just form of government. The effects of fake news and its proliferation can be felt at local and global levels, from ruining individual lives to shifting geopolitical balance.

Fake news is not technically a new phenomenon, although it has been enjoying a kind of renaissance in the past couple of years. There have been periods in the past during which journalism became trashy and sensationalist. What makes the twenty-first century different? Technology. The influence of fake news on government and society has grown with every new technological advance. This book will give you a deeper understanding of what fake news is, its impact on local and global events, the psychological and political purposes of fake news, and how fake news is often fueled by the pursuit of profit and power.

CHAPTER 1

Making Fake News

In the world of fake news, creators almost always have some plan. The plan might be to make money: on average, fake news is more popular and more viral than real news. It's more exciting, which means more views, more shares, and more ad revenue. The plan could also be political: fake news can convince people of something that will make them appreciate or reject a prominent politician, or even simply plant the seeds of doubt. Whatever the plan, whether the creators are entrepreneurial jokers or organized propaganda machines, fake news has real world consequences.

Inside a Fake News Sausage Factory: 'This Is All About Income'

BY ANDREW HIGGINS, MIKE MCINTIRE AND GABRIEL J.X. DANCE | NOV. 25, 2016

TBILISI, GEORGIA — Jobless and with graduation looming, a computer science student at the premier university in the nation of Georgia decided early this year that money could be made from America's voracious appetite for passionately partisan political news. He set up a website, posted gushing stories about Hillary Clinton and waited for ad sales to soar.

"I don't know why, but it did not work," said the student, Beqa Latsabidze, 22, who was savvy enough to change course when he realized what did drive traffic: laudatory stories about Donald J. Trump that mixed real — and completely fake — news in a stew of anti-Clinton fervor.

More than 6,000 miles away in Vancouver, a Canadian who runs a satirical website, John Egan, had made a similar observation.

Mr. Egan's site, The Burrard Street Journal, offers sendups of the news, not fake news, and he is not trying to fool anyone. But he, too, discovered that writing about Mr. Trump was a "gold mine." His traffic soared and his work, notably a story that President Obama would move to Canada if Mr. Trump won, was plundered by Mr. Latsabidze and other internet entrepreneurs for their own websites.

"It's all Trump," Mr. Egan said by telephone. "People go nuts for it."

With Mr. Obama now warning of the corrosive threat from fake political news circulated on Facebook and other social media, the pressing question is who produces these stories, and how does this overheated, often fabricated news ecosystem work?

Some analysts worry that foreign intelligence agencies are meddling in American politics and using fake news to influence elections. But one window into how the meat in fake sausages gets ground can be found in the buccaneering internet economy, where satire produced in Canada can be taken by a recent college graduate in the former Soviet republic of Georgia and presented as real news to attract clicks from credulous readers in the United States. Mr. Latsabidze said his only incentive was to make money from Google ads by luring people off Facebook pages and onto his websites.

To gin up material, Mr. Latsabidze often simply cut and pasted, sometimes massaging headlines but mostly just copying material from elsewhere, including Mr. Egan's prank story on Mr. Obama. Mr. Egan was not amused to see his satirical work on Mr. Latsabidze's website and filed a copyright infringement notice to defend his intellectual property.

Yet Mr. Egan conceded a certain professional glee that Mr. Trump is here to stay. "Now that we've got him for four years," he said, "I can't believe it."

By some estimates, bogus news stories appearing online and on social media had an even greater reach in the final months of the presidential campaign than articles by mainstream news organizations.

SOUL SEARCHING

Since then, internet giants like Facebook and Google have engaged in soul searching over their roles in disseminating false news. Google announced that it would ban websites that host fake news from using its online advertising service, while Facebook's chief executive, Mark Zuckerberg, outlined some of the options his company was considering, including simpler ways for users to flag suspicious content.

In Tbilisi, the two-room rented apartment Mr. Latsabidze shares with his younger brother is an unlikely offshore outpost of America's fake news industry. The two brothers, both computer experts, get help from a third young Georgian, an architect.

They say they have no keen interest in politics themselves and initially placed bets across the American political spectrum and experimented with show business news, too. They set up a pro-Clinton website, walkwithher.com, a Facebook page cheering Bernie Sanders and a web digest of straightforward political news plagiarized from The New York Times and other mainstream news media.

But those sites, among the more than a dozen registered by Mr. Latsabidze, were busts. Then he shifted all his energy to Mr. Trump. His flagship pro-Trump website, departed.co, gained remarkable traction in a crowded field in the prelude to the Nov. 8 election thanks to a steady menu of relentlessly pro-Trump and anti-Clinton stories. (On Wednesday, a few hours after The New York Times met with Mr. Latsabidze to ask him about his activities, the site vanished along with his Facebook page.)

"My audience likes Trump," he said. "I don't want to write bad things about Trump. If I write fake stories about Trump, I lose my audience."

Some of his Trump stories are true, some are highly slanted and others are totally false, like one this summer reporting that "the Mexican government announced they will close their borders to Americans in the event that Donald Trump is elected President of the United States." Data compiled by BuzzFeed showed that the story was the third most-trafficked fake story on Facebook from May to July.

So successful was the formula that others in Georgia and other faraway lands joined in, too, including Nika Kurdadze, a college acquaintance of Mr. Latsabidze's who set up his own pro-Trump site, newsbreakshere.com. Its recent offerings included a fake report headlined: "Stop it Liberals...Hillary Lost the Popular Vote by Several Million. Here's Why." That story, like most of Mr. Latsabidze's work, was pilfered from the web.

Mr. Latsabidze initially ran into no problems from all his cutting and pasting of other people's stories, and he even got ripped off himself when a rival in India hijacked a pro-Trump Facebook page he had set up to drive traffic to his websites. (He said that the Indian rival had offered $10,000 to buy the page, but that he had reneged on payment after being provided with access rights and commandeered it for himself.)

Then the notice arrived from Mr. Egan in Canada, which prompted the company that hosts Mr. Latsabidze's websites, including departed.co, to shut them down for two days until he removed the offending story.

"It was really bad for me," Mr. Latsabidze recalled. "Traffic dropped and I had to start everything all over again."

Mr. Egan, for his part, said he did not like others making money unfairly off his labor. And he estimated that "probably half" the readers of his stories believe they are true because of the widespread theft by other websites.

"A lot of that was conservative readers who see it picked up on other sites and believe it," Mr. Egan said. "In many cases, they haven't actually read it, they're just reacting to a headline."

FORM OF INFOTAINMENT

Mr. Latsabidze said he was amazed that anyone could mistake many of the articles he posts for real news.

"I don't call it fake news; I call it satire," he said. He avoids sex and violence because they violate Facebook rules, he said, but he sees nothing wrong otherwise with providing readers with what they want.

"Nobody really believes that Mexico is going to close its border," he said, sipping coffee this week in a McDonald's in downtown Tbilisi. "This is crazy."

All the same, the Mexico-closing-its-border story proved so popular after it appeared on his site that he hunted around on the web for other articles on the same theme. He found a tall tale about Mexico planning to call back its citizens from the United States if Mr. Trump won. This, too, generated huge traffic, though not quite as much as the first one, which Mr. Latsabidze described as "a really great story."

He insisted he has nothing against Mexicans or Muslims, whose exclusion from the United States is requested by an online petition that often appears on his websites and who are invariably presented in a negative light in the stories he posts.

"I am not against Muslims," he said. "I just saw that there was interest. They are in the news." Nor, he added, is he particularly against Mrs. Clinton, though he personally prefers Mr. Trump.

If his pro-Clinton site had taken off, he said, he would have pressed on with that, but "people did not engage," so he focused on serving pro-Trump supporters instead. They, he quickly realized, were a far more receptive audience "because they are angry" and eager to read outrageous tales.

"For me, this is all about income, nothing more," he added.

The income comes mostly from Google, which pays a few cents each time a reader sees or clicks on advertisements embedded in one of Mr. Latsabidze's websites. His best month, which coincided with the hit bogus story about Mexico closing the border, brought in around $6,000, though monthly revenue is usually much lower.

Mr. Obama, speaking in Berlin last week, assailed the spread of phony news on Facebook and other platforms, warning that "if we are not serious about facts and what's true and what's not" and "if we can't discriminate between serious arguments and propaganda, then we have problems."

While Facebook does not directly provide Mr. Latsabidze any revenue, it plays a central role in driving traffic to his websites. He initially established several fake Facebook pages intended to steer traffic to his websites, including one supposedly set up by a beautiful woman named Valkiara Beka. This woman, he acknowledged, does not really exist. "She is me," he said.

He discovered, however, that such pages were ineffective compared with legitimate Facebook pages from real people, particularly Trump supporters, because they have so much energy and love promoting stories they like.

Departed.co — named after Mr. Latsabidze's favorite movie, "The Departed," and recently redirected to usatodaycom.com — published dozens of stories daily, many of them similar to one posted on Nov. 17 with the headline, "This Is Huuge! International Arrest Warrant Issued By Putin For George Soros!" The story was not true and had already been published on scores of other fake news sites around the web.

Then there are the stories that have a grain of truth, along with big dollops of exaggeration and extrapolation, like "Dying Hillary Says She Just Wants To Curl Up And Never Leave Her House Again After Defeat." Mrs. Clinton did say the day after her election defeat that she just wanted to curl up with a book. But she was not, as far as anyone knows, dying.

KREMLIN SUSPICIONS

In the prelude to the election, bogus reports about Mrs. Clinton's health and highly favorable ones about Mr. Trump were promoted with gusto by Russian state-controlled news media outlets and legions of pro-Russian internet agitators. This has stirred suspicions that the Kremlin has had a hand in the fake news industry, prompting American researchers to assert in recent studies that the online blurring of the boundary between truth and falsehood is in part the result of Russian manipulation.

But Mr. Latsabidze and others here say they serve only their bank balances, not Russia or anything else.

He insisted that his team operated entirely on its own and that it did not want or need outside help. He said that it took him just two hours to set up a basic website and that anyone with a modicum of computer savvy could quickly start hawking news — real or fake — online.

"I did not invent anything," he said. "It has all been done before."

Mr. Latsabidze, who apparently has broken no laws, said that any crackdown on fake news might work in the short term but that "something else will come along to replace it."

"If they want to, they can control everything," he said, "but this will stop freedom of speech."

For now, the postelection period has been bad for business, with a sharp fall in the appetite for incendiary political news favoring Mr. Trump. Traffic to departed.co and affiliated websites has plunged in recent weeks by at least 50 percent, Mr. Latsabidze said.

"If Hillary had won, it would be better for us," he said. "I could write about the bad things she was going to do," he said. "I did not write to make Trump win. I just wanted to get viewers and make some money."

In the months since he got into the fake news business, Mr. Latsabidze has landed a day job as a programmer with a software company, which he sees as a better future. "This is more stable work," he said.

But he seemed reluctant to quit altogether.

"Are there any elections coming up in the U.K.?" Mr. Latsabidze asked.

He was disappointed to hear that none were scheduled soon. But, advised that France will hold a hotly contested presidential election next April featuring a Trump-like candidate in the form of Marine Le Pen, a far-right populist, he perked up.

"Maybe I should learn some French," he said.

How Fiction Becomes Fact on Social Media

BY BENEDICT CAREY | OCT. 20, 2017

HOURS AFTER THE Las Vegas massacre, Travis McKinney's Facebook feed was hit with a scattershot of conspiracy theories. The police were lying. There were multiple shooters in the hotel, not just one. The sheriff was covering for casino owners to preserve their business.

The political rumors sprouted soon after, like digital weeds. The killer was anti-Trump, an "antifa" activist, said some; others made the opposite claim, that he was an alt-right terrorist. The two unsupported narratives ran into the usual stream of chatter, news and selfies.

"This stuff was coming in from all over my network of 300 to 400" friends and followers, said Mr. McKinney, 52, of Suffolk, Va., and some posts were from his inner circle.

But he knew there was only one shooter; a handgun instructor and defense contractor, he had been listening to the police scanner in Las Vegas with an app. "I jumped online and tried to counter some of this nonsense," he said.

In the coming weeks, executives from Facebook and Twitter will appear before congressional committees to answer questions about the use of their platforms by Russian hackers and others to spread misinformation and skew elections. During the 2016 presidential campaign, Facebook sold more than $100,000 worth of ads to a Kremlin-linked company, and Google sold more than $4,500 worth to accounts thought to be connected to the Russian government.

Agents with links to the Russian government set up an endless array of fake accounts and websites and purchased a slew of advertisements on Google and Facebook, spreading dubious claims that seemed intended to sow division all along the political spectrum — "a cultural hack," in the words of one expert.

STEPHEN SAVAGE

Yet the psychology behind social media platforms — the dynamics that make them such powerful vectors of misinformation in the first place — is at least as important, experts say, especially for those who think they're immune to being duped. For all the suspicions about social media companies' motives and ethics, it is the interaction of the technology with our common, often subconscious psychological biases that makes so many of us vulnerable to misinformation, and this has largely escaped notice.

Skepticism of online "news" serves as a decent filter much of the time, but our innate biases allow it to be bypassed, researchers have found — especially when presented with the right kind of algorithmically selected "meme."

At a time when political misinformation is in ready supply, and in demand, "Facebook, Google, and Twitter function as a distribution mechanism, a platform for circulating false information and helping find receptive audiences," said Brendan Nyhan, a professor of government at Dartmouth College (and occasional contributor to The Times's Upshot column).

For starters, said Colleen Seifert, a professor of psychology at the University of Michigan, "People have a benevolent view of Facebook, for instance, as a curator, but in fact it does have a motive of its own. What it's actually doing is keeping your eyes on the site. It's curating news and information that will keep you watching."

That kind of curating acts as a fertile host for falsehoods by simultaneously engaging two predigital social-science standbys: the urban myth as "meme," or viral idea; and individual biases, the automatic, subconscious presumptions that color belief.

The first process is largely data-driven, experts said, and built into social media algorithms. The wide circulation of bizarre, easily debunked rumors — so-called Pizzagate, for example, the canard that Hillary Clinton was running a child sex ring from a Washington-area pizza parlor — is not entirely dependent on partisan fever (though that was its origin).

For one, the common wisdom that these rumors gain circulation because most people conduct their digital lives in echo chambers or "information cocoons" is exaggerated, Dr. Nyhan said.

In a forthcoming paper, Dr. Nyhan and colleagues review the relevant research, including analyses of partisan online news sites and Nielsen data, and find the opposite. Most people are more omnivorous than presumed; they are not confined in warm bubbles containing only agreeable outrage.

But they don't have to be for fake news to spread fast, research also suggests. Social media algorithms function at one level like evolutionary selection: Most lies and false rumors go nowhere, but the rare ones with appealing urban-myth "mutations" find psychological traction, then go viral.

There is no precise formula for such digital catnip. The point, experts said, is that the very absurdity of the Pizzagate lie could have boosted its early prominence, no matter the politics of those who shared it.

"My experience is that once this stuff gets going, people just pass these stories on without even necessarily stopping to read them," Mr.

McKinney said. "They're just participating in the conversation without stopping to look hard" at the source.

Digital social networks are "dangerously effective at identifying memes that are well adapted to surviving, and these also tend to be the rumors and conspiracy theories that are hardest to correct," Dr. Nyhan said.

One reason is the raw pace of digital information sharing, he said: "The networks make information run so fast that it outruns fact-checkers' ability to check it. Misinformation spreads widely before it can be downgraded in the algorithms."

The extent to which Facebook and other platforms function as "marketers" of misinformation, similar to the way they market shoes and makeup, is contentious. In 2015, a trio of behavior scientists working at Facebook inflamed the debate in a paper published in the prominent journal Science.

The authors analyzed the news feeds of some 10 million users in the United States who posted their political views, and concluded that "individuals' choices played a stronger role in limiting exposure" to contrary news and commentary than Facebook's own algorithmic ranking — which gauges how interesting stories are likely to be to individual users, based on data they have provided.

Outside critics lashed the study as self-serving, while other researchers said the analysis was solid and without apparent bias.

The other dynamic that works in favor of proliferating misinformation is not embedded in the software but in the biological hardware: the cognitive biases of the human brain.

Purely from a psychological point of view, subtle individual biases are at least as important as rankings and choice when it comes to spreading bogus news or Russian hoaxes — like a false report of Muslim men in Michigan collecting welfare for multiple wives.

Merely understanding what a news report or commentary is saying requires a temporary suspension of disbelief. Mentally, the reader must temporarily accept the stated "facts" as possibly true. A cognitive connection is made automatically: Clinton-sex offender, Trump-Nazi, Muslim men-welfare.

STEPHEN SAVAGE

And refuting those false claims requires a person to first mentally articulate them, reinforcing a subconscious connection that lingers far longer than people presume.

Over time, for many people, it is that false initial connection that stays the strongest, not the retractions or corrections: "Was Obama a Muslim? I seem to remember that...."

In a recent analysis of the biases that help spread misinformation, Dr. Seifert and co-authors named this and several other automatic cognitive connections that can buttress false information.

Another is repetition: Merely seeing a news headline multiple times in a news feed makes it seem more credible before it is ever read carefully, even if it's a fake item being whipped around by friends as a joke.

And, as salespeople have known forever, people tend to value the information and judgments offered by good friends over all other sources. It's a psychological tendency with significant consequences now that nearly two-thirds of Americans get at least some of their news from social media.

“Your social alliances affect how you weight information,” said Dr. Seifert. “We overweight information from people we know.”

The casual, social, wisecracking nature of thumbing through and participating in the digital exchanges allows these biases to operate all but unchecked, Dr. Seifert said.

Stopping to drill down and determine the true source of a foul-smelling story can be tricky, even for the motivated skeptic, and mentally it’s hard work. Ideological leanings and viewing choices are conscious, downstream factors that come into play only after automatic cognitive biases have already had their way, abetted by the algorithms and social nature of digital interactions.

“If I didn’t have direct evidence that all these theories were wrong” from the scanner, Mr. McKinney said, “I might have taken them a little more seriously.”

From Headline to Photograph, a Fake News Masterpiece

BY SCOTT SHANE | JAN. 18, 2017

ANNAPOLIS, MD. — It was early fall, and Donald J. Trump, behind in the polls, seemed to be preparing a rationale in case a winner like him somehow managed to lose. "I'm afraid the election is going to be rigged, I have to be honest," the Republican nominee told a riled-up crowd in Columbus, Ohio. He was hearing "more and more" about evidence of rigging, he added, leaving the details to his supporters' imagination.

A few weeks later, Cameron Harris, a new college graduate with a fervent interest in Maryland Republican politics and a need for cash, sat down at the kitchen table in his apartment to fill in the details

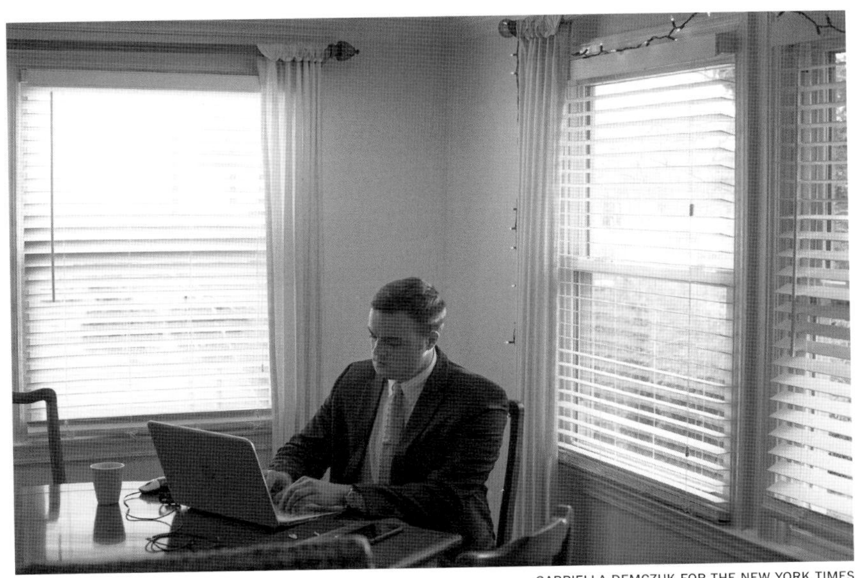

GABRIELLA DEMCZUK FOR THE NEW YORK TIMES

Cameron Harris in his home office in Annapolis, Md., on Monday. He created a fake story about an electrical worker who stumbled upon stacked boxes of ballots pre-marked for Hillary Clinton.

Mr. Trump had left out. In a dubious art just coming into its prime, this bogus story would be his masterpiece.

Mr. Harris started by crafting the headline: "BREAKING: 'Tens of thousands' of fraudulent Clinton votes found in Ohio warehouse." It made sense, he figured, to locate this shocking discovery in the very city and state where Mr. Trump had highlighted his "rigged" meme. "I had a theory when I sat down to write it," recalled Mr. Harris, a 23-year-old former college quarterback and fraternity leader. "Given the severe distrust of the media among Trump supporters, anything that parroted Trump's talking points people would click. Trump was saying 'rigged election, rigged election.' People were predisposed to believe Hillary Clinton could not win except by cheating."

In a raucous election year defined by made-up stories, Mr. Harris was a home-grown, self-taught practitioner, a boutique operator with no ties to Russian spy agencies or Macedonian fabrication factories. As Mr. Trump takes office this week, the beneficiary of at least a modest electoral boost from a flood of fakery, Mr. Harris and his ersatz-news website, ChristianTimesNewspaper.com, make for an illuminating tale.

Contacted by a reporter who had discovered an electronic clue that revealed his secret authorship of ChristianTimesNewspaper.com, he was wary at first, chagrined to be unmasked.

"This topic is rather sensitive," Mr. Harris said, noting that he was trying to build a political consulting business and needed to protect his reputation. But eventually he agreed to tell the story of his foray into fake news, a very part-time gig that he calculated paid him about $1,000 an hour in web advertising revenue. He seemed to regard his experience with a combination of guilt about having spread falsehoods and pride at doing it so skillfully.

At his kitchen table that night in September, Mr. Harris wondered: Who might have found these fraudulent Clinton ballots? So he invented "Randall Prince, a Columbus-area electrical worker." This Everyman, a "Trump supporter" whose name hinted at a sort of nobility, had entered a little-used back room at the warehouse and stumbled upon stacked boxes of ballots pre-marked for Mrs. Clinton, Mr. Harris decided.

"No one really goes in this building. It's mainly used for short-term storage by a commercial plumber," Prince said.

In case anyone missed the significance of the find, Mr. Harris made it plain: "What he found could allegedly be evidence of a massive operation designed to deliver Clinton the crucial swing state."

A photograph, he thought, would help erase doubts about his yarn. With a quick Google image search for "ballot boxes," he landed on a shot of a balding fellow standing behind black plastic boxes that helpfully had "Ballot Box" labels.

It was a photo from The Birmingham Mail, showing a British election 3,700 miles from Columbus — but no matter. In the caption, the balding Briton got a new name: "Mr. Prince, shown here, poses with his find, as election officials investigate."

The article explained that "the Clinton campaign's likely goal was to slip the fake ballot boxes in with the real ballot boxes when they went to official election judges on November 8th." Then Mr. Harris added a touch of breathlessness.

"This story is still developing," he wrote, "and CTN will bring you more when we have it."

He pushed the button and the story was launched on Sept. 30, blazing across the web like some kind of counterfeit comet. "Even before I posted it, I knew it would take off," Mr. Harris recalled.

He was correct. The ballot box story, promoted by a half-dozen Facebook pages Mr. Harris had created for the purpose, flew around the web, fueled by indignant comments from people who were certain that Mrs. Clinton was going to cheat Mr. Trump of victory and who welcomed the proof. It was eventually shared with six million people, according to CrowdTangle, which tracks web audiences.

BREAKING: "Tens of thousands" of fraudulent Clinton votes found in Ohio warehouse https://t.co/yU1AyAVRHp via @ FoxNews @ @CBSNews @ABC

— TRUMP TV® (@SJavner) Oct. 2, 2016

The next day, the Franklin County, Ohio, board of elections announced that it was investigating and that the fraud claims appeared to be untrue. Within days, Ohio's secretary of state, Jon Husted, issued a statement to deny the story.

"A Christian myself, I take offense to reading such unbelievable lies from a publication alleging Christian ties," Mr. Husted said.

There was nothing especially Christian about his efforts, Mr. Harris admits; he had simply bought the abandoned web address for $5 at ExpiredDomains.net. Within a few days, the story, which had taken him 15 minutes to concoct, had earned him about $5,000. That was a sizable share of the $22,000 an accounting statement shows he made during the presidential campaign from ads for shoes, hair gel and web design that Google had placed on his site.

He had put in perhaps half an hour a week on the fake news site, he said, for a total of about 20 hours. He would come close to a far bigger payday, one that might have turned the $5 he had spent on the Christian Times domain into more than $100,000.

The money, not the politics, was the point, he insisted. He had graduated from Davidson College in North Carolina in May, and he needed to pay his living expenses. "I spent the money on student loans, car payments and rent," he said.

By the time he launched his fraudulent story on ballot fraud, he had found minimal success with "Hillary Clinton Blames Racism for Cincinnati Gorilla's Death," a reference to the sad tale of Harambe, the gorilla shot after he grabbed a little boy visiting the zoo. He had done better with "Early Morning Explosion in DC Allegedly Leaves Yet Another DNC Staffer Dead," spinning off conspiracy theories around the earlier shooting death of a Democratic National Committee staff member.

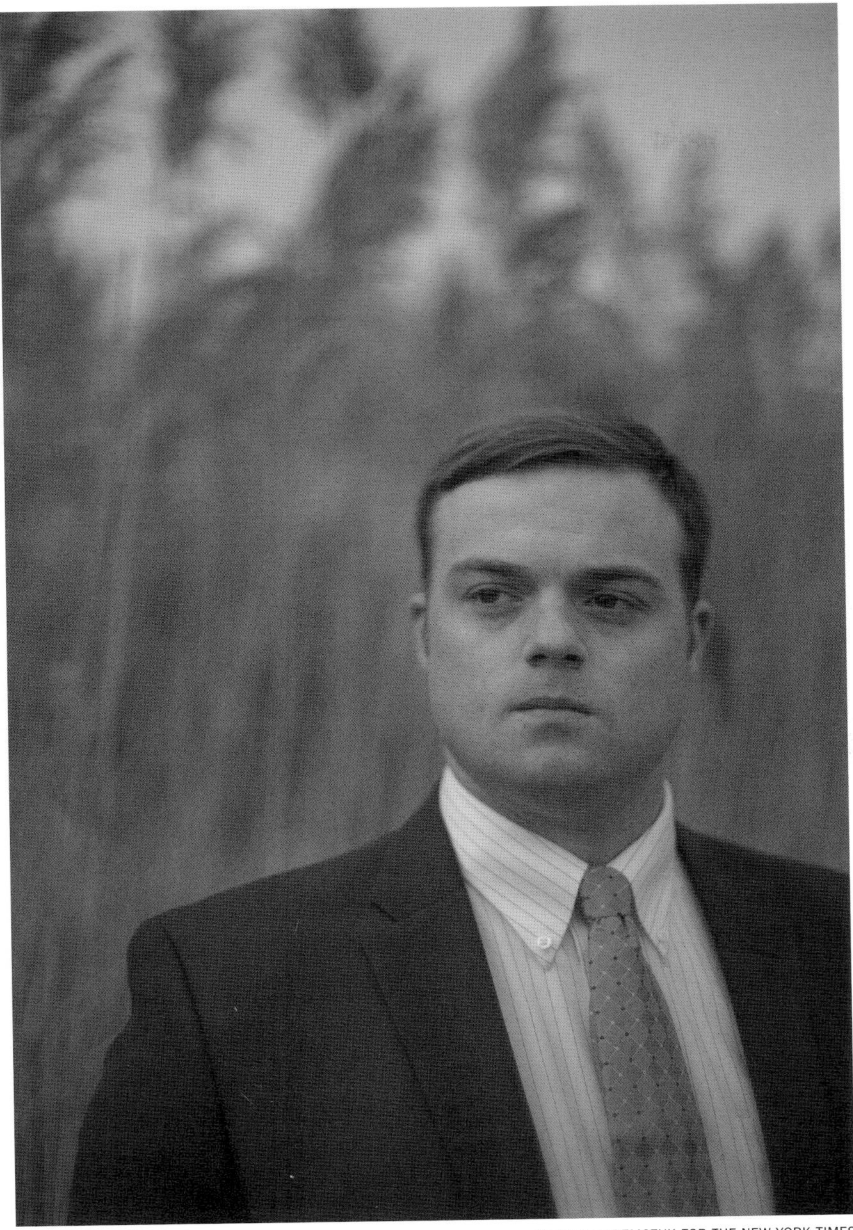

GABRIELLA DEMCZUK FOR THE NEW YORK TIMES

"At first it kind of shocked me — the response I was getting," Mr. Harris said. "How easily people would believe it. It was almost like a sociological experiment."

Later, he would tell gullible readers "NYPD Looking to Press Charges Against Bill Clinton for Underage Sex Ring," "Protesters Beat Homeless Veteran to Death in Philadelphia" and "Hillary Clinton Files for Divorce in New York Courts." Eight of his stories would merit explicit debunking by Snopes.com, the myth-busting site, but none would top the performance of the ballot box fantasy.

President Obama thought the fake news phenomenon significant enough to mention it as a threat to democracy in his farewell speech in Chicago last week. "Increasingly," he said, "we become so secure in our bubbles that we start accepting only information, whether it's true or not, that fits our opinions, instead of basing our opinions on the evidence that is out there."

That was exactly the insight on which Mr. Harris said he built his transient business: that people wanted to be fed evidence, however implausible, to support their beliefs. "At first it kind of shocked me — the response I was getting," he said. "How easily people would believe it. It was almost like a sociological experiment," added Mr. Harris, who majored in political science and economics.

By his account, though he voted for Mr. Trump, his early preference had been for Senator Marco Rubio. Mr. Harris said he would have been willing to promote Mrs. Clinton and smear Mr. Trump had those tactics been lucrative. But as other seekers of clicks discovered, Mr. Trump's supporters were far more fervent than Mrs. Clinton's.

In late October, with the inevitable end of his venture approaching, Mr. Harris sought an appraisal for the web domain that by then had vaulted into the web's top 20,000 sites. An appraiser said that given the traffic, he could probably sell it for between $115,000 and $125,000.

But Mr. Harris made a costly mistake: He decided to wait. Days after the election, denounced for making the peddling of fake news remunerative, Google announced that it would no longer place ads on sites promoting clearly fabricated stories.

A few days later, when Mr. Harris checked his site, the ads were gone. He checked with the appraiser and was told that the domain was now essentially worthless.

All was not lost, however. He had put a pop-up on the site inviting visitors to “join the ‘Stop the Steal’ team to find out HOW Hillary plans to steal the election and what YOU can do to stop her!” and collected 24,000 email addresses. He has not yet decided what to do with them, he said.

Asked whether he felt any guilt at having spread lies about a presidential candidate, Mr. Harris grew thoughtful. But he took refuge in the notion that politics is by its nature replete with exaggerations, half-truths and outright whoppers, so he was hardly adding much to the sum total.

“Hardly anything a campaign or a candidate says is completely true,” he said.

Lately he has picked up Mr. Trump’s refrain that mainstream news organizations are themselves regular purveyors of fake news. Last week, when BuzzFeed released what it called an “explosive but unverified” dossier suggesting that Russia had planned to bribe and blackmail Mr. Trump, Mr. Harris wrote on Twitter:

“Explosive but unverified”

That could describe every fake news headline ever. https://t.co/hj5fgvVfHn

— Cam Harris (@camharris_us) Jan. 11, 2017

He did not mention his own expertise in the field.

How to Fight 'Fake News' (Warning: It Isn't Easy)

BY NIRAJ CHOKSHI | SEPT. 18, 2017

NO, THE REESE'S Peanut Butter Cup is not being discontinued. No, Earth will not be plunged into darkness for 15 days. And, no, Katy Perry did not broker peace with the Islamic State.

Those are a few of the falsehoods spread online that are in need of debunking in this age of "fake news," when misinformation seems to appear from nothing and reaches hurricane-force speeds in an instant.

Researchers have spent decades trying to understand how such misinformation spreads and, now, a review of their work offers new guidance for the journalists, fact-checkers and others working to find, and defend, the truth.

In a report published last week in Psychological Science, a team of academics reviewed two decades of research to better understand how to effectively debunk misinformation. In the end, they found eight worthwhile studies, with more than 6,800 participants.

Based on the findings of those experiments, the authors offer these broad recommendations for how to expose misinformation.

LIMIT ARGUMENTS SUPPORTING MISINFORMATION

If you have to repeat a lie, it's best to limit the description of it, said Kathleen Hall Jamieson, one of the study's authors, who is also the director of the Annenberg Public Policy Center at the University of Pennsylvania and a founder of FactCheck.org.

The problem, she and the other authors said, is that rehashing arguments in favor of misinformation can inadvertently reinforce it, strengthening the defense against the truth.

That's especially true when the lie offers a simpler explanation than the truth, as with the discredited argument linking the vaccine against measles, mumps and rubella to the onset of autism.

STEPHEN CROWLEY/THE NEW YORK TIMES

Donald J. Trump with President Barack Obama at the White House in November, soon after the presidential election. For years, Mr. Trump promoted the false claim that Mr. Obama was not born in the United States.

"The best way to displace that would be to say, 'Here's a causal explanation for autism, and it isn't that,' but science doesn't know the causal explanation for autism yet," Ms. Jamieson said.

With no alternative to replace it, the discredited theory proves remarkably resilient. And repeating the arguments in the theory's favor only make it stickier, she said.

ENCOURAGE SCRUTINY

When debunking information, it's also useful to get the audience in a skeptical mind-set, the authors argue.

Take the widely refuted "birther" theory — promoted for years by President Trump — which suggests that President Barack Obama, was not, in fact, born in the United States. Just labeling the theory "false" is not as convincing to people who believe it as walking them through the reasons it can't be true, Ms. Jamieson said.

PAUL PORTER/PATRICK MCMULLAN VIA GETTY IMAGES

Kathleen Hall Jamieson, an author of a new report on how to debunk misinformation, at the WEBBY Awards in 2007.

It's also helpful to make the audience feel engaged with the skepticism, said Dolores Albarracín, an author of the paper and a professor of psychology, business and medicine at the University of Illinois at Urbana-Champaign.

"You lead them down the garden path rather than do all the work for them," she said.

PRESENT NEW INFORMATION

Giving your audience new and credible information is especially effective in thoroughly unseating misinformation, the authors found.

That, they said, supports their hypothesis that the new information allows people to update their understanding of events, justifying why they fell for the falsehood in the first place.

BONUS: VIDEO MAY WORK BETTER THAN TEXT

In a study published this summer in Journalism & Mass Communication Quarterly, Ms. Jamieson and three other authors found that videos could be especially useful in correcting misinformation. The fact-checking videos seemed to "increase attention and reduce confusion" compared with text, one of the authors said in a statement at the time.

Here Come the Fake Videos, Too

BY KEVIN ROOSE | MARCH 4, 2018

Artificial intelligence video tools make it relatively easy to put one person's face on another person's body with few traces of manipulation. I tried it on myself. What could go wrong?

THE SCENE OPENED on a room with a red sofa, a potted plant and the kind of bland modern art you'd see on a therapist's wall.

In the room was Michelle Obama, or someone who looked exactly like her. Wearing a low-cut top with a black bra visible underneath, she writhed lustily for the camera and flashed her unmistakable smile.

Then, the former first lady's doppelgänger began to strip.

The video, which appeared on the online forum Reddit, was what's known as a "deepfake" — an ultrarealistic fake video made with artificial intelligence software. It was created using a program called FakeApp, which superimposed Mrs. Obama's face onto the body of a pornographic film actress. The hybrid was uncanny — if you didn't know better, you might have thought it was really her.

Until recently, realistic computer-generated video was a laborious pursuit available only to big-budget Hollywood productions or cutting-edge researchers. Social media apps like Snapchat include some rudimentary face-morphing technology.

But in recent months, a community of hobbyists has begun experimenting with more powerful tools, including FakeApp — a program that was built by an anonymous developer using open-source software written by Google. FakeApp makes it free and relatively easy to create realistic face swaps and leave few traces of manipulation. Since a version of the app appeared on Reddit in January, it has been downloaded more than 120,000 times, according to its creator.

Deepfakes are one of the newest forms of digital media manipulation, and one of the most obviously mischief-prone. It's not hard to imagine this technology's being used to smear politicians, create counterfeit revenge porn or frame people for crimes. Lawmakers have already begun to worry about how deepfakes could be used for political sabotage and propaganda.

Even on morally lax sites like Reddit, deepfakes have raised eyebrows. Recently, FakeApp set off a panic after Motherboard, the technology site, reported that people were using it to create pornographic deepfakes of celebrities. Pornhub, Twitter and other sites quickly banned the videos, and Reddit closed a handful of deepfake groups, including one with nearly 100,000 members.

Before the Reddit deepfake groups were closed, they hosted a mixture of users trading video-editing tips and showing off their latest forgeries. A post titled "3D face reconstruction for additional angles" sat next to videos with titles like "(Not) Olivia Wilde playing with herself."

Some users on Reddit defended deepfakes and blamed the media for overhyping their potential for harm. Others moved their videos to alternative platforms, rightly anticipating that Reddit would crack down under its rules against nonconsensual pornography. And a few expressed moral qualms about putting the technology into the world.

Then, they kept making more.

The deepfake creator community is now in the internet's shadows. But while out in the open, it gave an unsettling peek into the future.

"This is turning into an episode of Black Mirror," wrote one Reddit user. The post raised the ontological questions at the heart of the deepfake debate: Does a naked image of Person A become a naked image of Person B if Person B's face is superimposed in a seamless and untraceable way? In a broader sense, on the internet, what is the difference between representation and reality?

The user then signed off with a shrug: "Godspeed rebels."

MAKING DEEPFAKES

After lurking for several weeks in Reddit's deepfake community, I decided to see how easy it was to create a (safe for work, nonpornographic) deepfake using my own face.

I started by downloading FakeApp and enlisting two technical experts to help me. The first was Mark McKeague, a colleague in The New York Times's research and development department. The second was a deepfake creator I found through Reddit, who goes by the nickname Derpfakes.

Because of the controversial nature of deepfakes, Derpfakes would not give his or her real name. Derpfakes started posting deepfake videos on YouTube a few weeks ago, specializing in humorous offerings like Nicolas Cage playing Superman. The account has also posted some how-to videos on deepfake creation.

What I learned is that making a deepfake isn't simple. But it's not rocket science, either.

The first step is to find, or rent, a moderately powerful computer. FakeApp uses a suite of machine learning tools called TensorFlow, which was developed by Google's A.I. division and released to the public in 2015. The software teaches itself to perform image-recognition tasks through trial and error. The more processing power on hand, the faster it works.

To get more speed, Mark and I used a remote server rented through Google Cloud Platform. It provided enough processing power to cut the time frame down to hours, rather than the days or weeks it might take on my laptop.

Once Mark set up the remote server and loaded FakeApp on it, we were on to the next step: data collection.

Picking the right source data is crucial. Short video clips are easier to manipulate than long clips, and scenes shot at a single angle produce better results than scenes with multiple angles. Genetics also help. The more the faces resemble each other, the better.

I'm a brown-haired white man with a short beard, so Mark and I decided to try several other brown-haired, stubbled white guys. We started with Ryan Gosling. (Aim high, right?) I also sent Derpfakes, my outsourced Reddit expert, several video options to choose from.

Next, we took several hundred photos of my face, and gathered images of Mr. Gosling's face using a clip from a recent TV appearance. FakeApp uses these images to train the deep learning model and teach it to emulate our facial expressions.

To get the broadest photo set possible, I twisted my head at different angles, making as many different faces as I could.

Mark then used a program to crop those images down, isolating just our faces, and manually deleted any blurred or badly cropped photos. He then fed the frames into FakeApp. In all, we used 417 photos of me, and 1,113 of Mr. Gosling.

When the images were ready, Mark pressed "start" on FakeApp, and the training began. His computer screen filled with images of my face and Mr. Gosling's face, as the program tried to identify patterns and similarities.

About eight hours later, after our model had been sufficiently trained, Mark used FakeApp to finish putting my face on Mr. Gosling's body. The video was blurry and bizarre, and Mr. Gosling's face occasionally flickered into view. Only the legally blind would mistake the person in the video for me.

We did better with a clip of Chris Pratt, the scruffy star of "Jurassic World," whose face shape is a little more similar to mine. For this test, Mark used a bigger data set — 1,861 photos of me, 1,023 of him — and let the model run overnight.

A few days later, Derpfakes, who had also been training a model, sent me a finished deepfake made using the footage I had sent and a video of the actor Jake Gyllenhaal. This one was much more lifelike, a true hybrid that mixed my facial features with his hair, beard and body.

Derpfakes repeated the process with videos of Jimmy Kimmel and Liev Schreiber, both of which turned out well. As an experienced deepfake creator, Derpfakes had a more intuitive sense of which source videos would produce a clean result, and more experience with the subtle blending and tweaking that takes place at the end of the deepfake process.

In all, our deepfake experiment took three days and cost $85.96 in Google Cloud Platform credits. That seemed like a small price to pay for stardom.

WHAT THE APP'S CREATOR SAYS

After the experiment, I reached out to the anonymous creator of FakeApp through an email address on its website. I wanted to know how it felt to create a cutting-edge A.I. tool, only to have it gleefully co-opted by ethically challenged pornographers.

A man wrote back, identifying himself as a software developer in Maryland. Like Derpfakes, the man would not give me his full name, and instead went by his first initial, N. He said he had created FakeApp as a creative experiment and was chagrined to see Reddit's deepfake community use it for ill.

"I joined the community based around these algorithms when it was very small (less than 500 people)," he wrote, "and as soon as I saw the results I knew this was brilliant tech that should be accessible to anyone who wants to play around with it. I figured I'd take a shot at putting together an easy-to-use package to accomplish that."

N. said he didn't support the use of FakeApp to create nonconsensual pornography or other abusive content. And he said he agreed with Reddit's decision to ban explicit deepfakes. But he defended the product.

"I've given it a lot of thought," he said, "and ultimately I've decided I don't think it's right to condemn the technology itself — which can of course be used for many purposes, good and bad."

FakeApp is somewhat finicky and hard to use, but it's easy to imagine it improving quickly. N. said that in the future, FakeApp could be used by all kinds of people to bring high-budget special effects to their personal projects.

Deep learning algorithms, he added, were going to be important in the future, not only as stand-alone apps but as powerful components of many tech products.

"It's precisely the things that make them so powerful and useful that make them so scary," he said. "There's really no limit to what you can apply it to with a little imagination."

'NEXT FORM OF COMMUNICATION'

On the day of the school shooting last month in Parkland, Fla., a screenshot of a BuzzFeed News article, "Why We Need to Take Away White People's Guns Now More Than Ever," written by a reporter named Richie Horowitz, began making the rounds on social media.

The whole thing was fake. No BuzzFeed employee named Richie Horowitz exists, and no article with that title was ever published on the site. But the doctored image pulsed through right-wing out-rage channels and was boosted by activists on Twitter. It wasn't an A.I.-generated deepfake, or even a particularly sophisticated Photoshop job, but it did the trick.

Online misinformation, no matter how sleekly produced, spreads through a familiar process once it enters our social distribution channels. The hoax gets 50,000 shares, and the debunking an hour later gets 200. The carnival barker gets an algorithmic boost on services like Facebook and YouTube, while the expert screams into the void.

There's no reason to believe that deepfake videos will operate any differently. People will share them when they're ideologically convenient and dismiss them when they're not. The dupes who fall for satirical stories from The Onion will be fooled by deepfakes, and the scrupulous people who care about the truth will find ways to detect and debunk them.

"There's no choice," said Hao Li, an assistant professor of computer science at the University of Southern California. Mr. Li, who is also the founder of Pinscreen, a company that uses artificial intelligence to create lifelike 3-D avatars, said the weaponization of A.I. was inevitable and would require a sudden shift in public awareness.

"I see this as the next form of communication," he said. "I worry that people will use it to blackmail others, or do bad things. You have to educate people that this is possible."

So, O.K. Here I am, telling you this: An A.I. program powerful enough to turn Michelle Obama into a pornography star, or transform a schlubby newspaper columnist into Jake Gyllenhaal, is in our midst. Manipulated video will soon become far more commonplace.

And there's probably nothing we can do except try to bat the fakes down as they happen, pressure social media companies to fight misinformation aggressively, and trust our eyes a little less every day.

Godspeed, rebels.

It's True: False News Spreads Faster and Wider. And Humans Are to Blame.

BY STEVE LOHR | MARCH 8, 2018

WHAT IF THE SCOURGE of false news on the internet is not the result of Russian operatives or partisan zealots or computer-controlled bots? What if the main problem is us?

People are the principal culprits, according to a new study examining the flow of stories on Twitter. And people, the study's authors also say, prefer false news.

As a result, false news travels faster, farther and deeper through the social network than true news.

The researchers, from the Massachusetts Institute of Technology, found that those patterns applied to every subject they studied, not only politics and urban legends, but also business, science and technology.

False claims were 70 percent more likely than the truth to be shared on Twitter. True stories were rarely retweeted by more than 1,000 people, but the top 1 percent of false stories were routinely shared by 1,000 to 100,000 people. And it took true stories about six times as long as false ones to reach 1,500 people.

Software robots can accelerate the spread of false stories. But the M.I.T. researchers, using software to identify and weed out bots, found that with or without the bots, the results were essentially the same.

"It's sort of disheartening at first to realize how much we humans are responsible," said Sinan Aral, a professor at the M.I.T. Sloan School of Management and an author of the study. "It's not really the robots that are to blame."

Here are other findings from the research.

COVERING THE HISTORY OF TWITTER

The research, published on Thursday in Science magazine, examined true and false news stories posted on Twitter from the social network's founding in 2006 through 2017. The study's authors tracked 126,000 stories tweeted by roughly three million people more than 4.5 million times. "News" and "stories" were defined broadly — as claims of fact — regardless of the source. And the study explicitly avoided the term "fake news," which, the authors write, has become "irredeemably polarized in our current political and media climate."

The stories were classified as true or false, using information from six independent fact-checking organizations including Snopes, PolitiFact and FactCheck.org. To ensure that their analysis held up in general — not just on claims that drew the attention of fact-checking groups — the researchers enlisted students to annotate as true or false more than 13,000 other stories that circulated on Twitter. Again, a tilt toward falsehood was clear.

MARK MAKELA FOR THE NEW YORK TIMES

Researchers at the Massachusetts Institute of Technology examined true and false news stories posted on Twitter from the social network's founding in 2006 through 2017.

The way information flows online — and, occasionally, spreads rapidly like a virus — has been studied for decades. There have also been smaller studies examining how true and false news and rumors propagate across social networks. But experts in network analysis said the M.I.T. study was larger in scale and well designed.

"The comprehensiveness is important here, spanning the entire history of Twitter," said Jon Kleinberg, a computer scientist at Cornell University. "And this study shines a spotlight on the open question of the success of false information online."

NOVELTY WINS RETWEETS

The M.I.T. researchers pointed to factors that contribute to the appeal of false news. Applying standard text-analysis tools, they found that false claims were significantly more novel than true ones — maybe not a surprise, since falsehoods are made up.

The study's authors also explored the emotions evoked by false and true stories. The goal, said Soroush Vosoughi, a postdoctoral researcher at the M.I.T. Media Lab and the lead author, was to find clues about what is "in the nature of humans that makes them like to share false news."

The study analyzed the sentiment expressed by users in replies to claims posted on Twitter. As a measurement tool, the researchers used a system created by Canada's National Research Council that associates English words with eight emotions. False claims elicited replies expressing greater surprise and disgust. True news inspired more anticipation, sadness and joy, depending on the nature of the stories.

TWO STORIES: ONE TRUE, ONE FALSE

The researchers provided an example of two business stories, and how much more time it took the true one to reach 200 retweets. The example also shows the judgment calls made by fact-checking organizations.

• In 2014, the fashion chain Zara introduced children's pajamas with horizontal stripes and a gold star. The company said the design was inspired by what a cowboy sheriff would wear. But Twitter users posted messages saying the pajamas resembled Nazi concentration camp uniforms. Snopes: True. Time to reach 200 retweets: 7.3 hours.

• In 2016, a website republished a portion of a satirical article about how the Chick-fil-A restaurant chain had decided to begin a "We don't like blacks either" marketing campaign to stir up controversy and boost sales. It came after the company's president did say he opposed gay marriage. Snopes: False. Time to 200 retweets: 4.2 hours.

WHAT CAN BE DONE?

The M.I.T. researchers said that understanding how false news spreads is a first step toward curbing it. They concluded that human behavior plays a large role in explaining the phenomenon, and mention possible interventions, like better labeling, to alter behavior.

For all the concern about false news, there is little certainty about its influence on people's beliefs and actions. A recent study of the browsing histories of thousands of American adults in the months before the 2016 election found that false news accounted for only a small portion of the total news people consumed. "We have to be very careful about making the inference that fake news has a big impact," said Duncan Watts, a principal researcher at Microsoft Research.

Another author of the M.I.T. study, Deb Roy, former chief media scientist at Twitter, is engaged in a project to improve the health of the information ecosystem. In fall 2016, Mr. Roy, an associate professor at the M.I.T. Media Lab, became a founder and the chairman of Cortico, a nonprofit that is developing tools to measure public conversations online to gauge attributes like shared attention, variety of opinion and receptivity. The idea is that improving the ability to measure such attributes would lead to better decision-making that would counteract misinformation.

Mr. Roy acknowledged the challenge in trying to not only alter individual behavior but also in enlisting the support of big internet platforms like Facebook, Google, YouTube and Twitter, and media companies.

"Polarization," he said, "has turned out to be a great business model."

For Fact-Checking Website Snopes, a Bigger Role Brings More Attacks

BY DAVID STREITFELD | DEC. 25, 2016

SAN DIEGO — The last line of defense against the torrent of half-truths, untruths and outright fakery that make up so much of the modern internet is in a downscale strip mall near the beach.

Snopes, the fact-checking website, does not have an office designed to impress, or even be noticed. A big sign outside still bears the name of the previous tenant, a maker of underwater headphones. Inside there's nothing much — a bunch of improvised desks, a table tennis table, cartons of Popchips and cases of Dr Pepper. It looks like a dot-com on the way to nowhere.

JOHN FRANCIS PETERS FOR THE NEW YORK TIMES

Brooke Binkowski, the managing editor of Snopes, in its office in San Diego. The idea that the website's work would slow down after the presidential election has proved unfounded.

Appearances deceive. This is where the muddled masses come by the virtual millions to establish just what the heck is really going on in a world turned upside down.

Did Donald J. Trump say on Twitter that he planned to arrest the "Saturday Night Live" star Alec Baldwin for sedition? Has Hillary Clinton quietly filed for divorce? Was Mr. Trump giving Kanye West a cabinet position? And was Alan Thicke, the star of "Growing Pains," really dead?

All untrue, except for the demise of Mr. Thicke, which was easily verifiable.

"Rationality seems to have fallen out of vogue," said Brooke Binkowski, Snopes's managing editor. "People don't know what to believe anymore. Everything is really strange right now."

That is certainly true at Snopes itself. For 20 years, the site was dedicated to urban legends, like the purported existence of alligators in New York City sewers, and other benign misinformation. But its range and readership increased significantly during a prolonged presidential election campaign in which the facts became a partisan issue and reality itself seemed up for grabs.

One way to chart Snopes's increasing prominence is by measuring the rise in fake news about the site itself. If you believe the internet, the founder of Snopes, David Mikkelson, has a longer rap sheet than Al Capone. He was supposedly arrested for committing fraud and corruption and running a pit bull ring. In the wake of a deal that Snopes and others made this month to start fact-checking for Facebook, new slurs and allegations poured forth.

The underlying message of these spurious attacks is that the movement to fact-check the internet is a left-wing conspiracy whose real goal is to censor the right, and therefore must be resisted at all costs.

"Smearing people just because you don't like what they're saying often works to shut them up," Ms. Binkowski, 39, said. "But at Snopes you learn to grow a thick skin. I will always push back. At least until someone shows up at my workplace and kills me."

Mr. Mikkelson, a former computer programmer, met his first wife, Barbara, in a folklore discussion group on the internet. They called their website Snopes in tribute to the venal family in William Faulkner's novels.

Their first group of posts, back in 1995, tackled questions about Disneyland, such as whether there really was a secret restaurant at the park. (There was.) It was a time when the nascent web was seen as a force that would deliver enlightenment and truth to all.

Starting about two years ago, Snopes made an effort to professionalize itself. It added a dozen staff members just in time to become the go-to debunking site for an election full of venom. The number of unique users jumped 42 percent over 2015, peaking at nearly 2.5 million the day after the election.

Just about everyone at Snopes thought things would calm down after the votes were in. "The fake news wasn't from Trump so much. It was from people who hated Hillary Clinton," Ms. Binkowski said. "Once the election was over we figured it would go away."

She scheduled a vacation, and thought she would spend more time writing about such things as how no one has a water bed anymore. Mr. Mikkelson, 56, went on a lengthy honeymoon in Japan and China.

But the role of fake news and misinformation in Mr. Trump's surprise win quickly reached a fever pitch, prompting questions about the extent to which Facebook, where many of these bogus stories were shared, had influenced the election. Reluctantly, the social media giant was forced to act.

The plan is for Facebook to send questionable links to a coalition of fact-checking sites, including Snopes. If the links are found to be dubious, Facebook will alert users by marking stories with a "disputed" designation.

Mr. Mikkelson, speaking from Washington State, declined to claim this new initiative was a potential turning point in the quest for truth on the internet, or even in the history of Snopes.

“I said, ‘O.K., we’ll give it a try,’ ” he said. “It doesn’t really involve us doing anything we wouldn’t already be doing.” As for Facebook, he thinks it had to do something but had few good options. Blocking content outright, for instance, would be a public relations minefield.

Even when he is in this country, Mr. Mikkelson is a bit elusive. His voice mail box is full, but he is in no hurry to clear it out. In the wake of a contentious divorce from Barbara, he now owns half of Snopes. The other half is owned by the principals of Proper Media, a digital media firm.

All of Snopes’s revenue — Mr. Mikkelson says he doesn’t know what it is — come from ads. Facebook is not paying for its services. Nor is the billionaire George Soros funding the site, although that is sometimes asserted in anti-Snopes stories.

Mr. Mikkelson seems more amused than outraged by the spectacle that is the internet, even when it takes aim at him.

“We don’t have any inflated sense of self-importance at Snopes,” he said. “People are always telling us, ‘You’re deviating from your mission.’ My response is: ‘We don’t have a mission. We just do what we do.’ ” But he conceded that something had gone wrong with the early utopian dreams for the internet.

“Making everyone equal as an information source doesn’t work very well in practice,” he said. Then he laughed, something he does frequently.

Ms. Binkowski, a former radio reporter who still freelances about border issues, thinks there is a mission.

“Not to be ideological or Pollyannaish, but you have to believe this work makes a difference,” she said. “Otherwise you’d just go back to bed and drink.” Although there are other benefits to working at Snopes: “I really like telling people they’re wrong.”

The Snopes writers generally take a long-term perspective on fake news. The practice itself they see as ancient. The difference now is that the stories circulate faster and people can make money spreading them, which gives its purveyors a whole new motivation.

There is also a cultural shift, said Kim LaCapria, who lives on Long Island and writes many of the Snopes political posts.

"It used to be that if you got too far from the mainstream, you were shunned for being a little nutty," she said. "Now there is so much nutty going around that it's socially acceptable to embrace wild accusations. No one is embarrassed by anything anymore."

The remedy, she and Ms. Binkowski feel, is more traditional journalism.

"People aren't necessarily getting the media literacy they need, so they're just kind of panicking," Ms. LaCapria said.

Mr. Thicke's death underlined this. In addition to those asking direct questions, thousands of users searched Snopes for confirmation of the actor's demise.

"People think the death of a 69-year-old from a heart attack must be a hoax. That is how muddy the waters are now," Ms. LaCapria said. "They are afraid, even with such an easily verifiable thing, to trust anyone."

But there are also those who trust too much, and they are a much larger group. The bios at the end of posts on Snopes are often whimsical, so Ms. LaCapria wrote that she got her job "due to an executive order unilaterally passed by President Obama during a secret, late-night session."

A joke — but her own mother took it at face value. "You've known me for 36 years. Of course it's not true!" Ms. LaCapria told her. "It's very easy for us to be tricked, all of us."

2004: When Fake News Was Cool

BY ALEX WILLIAMS | FEB. 9, 2018

Long before "fake news" became a cudgel for the Trumpites, it was the hippest form of protest for Jon Stewart types during the George W. Bush years.

2004 PRINT HEADLINE: "The Week That Wasn't," published here in October 2004.

The story: It was the year of fake news. No, not 2017, when so-called fake news reigned as a staple of the president's tweets, Facebook cracked down on false accounts that spewed propaganda, and Collins Dictionary anointed "fake news" its "word of the year."

Although the term has been co-opted as a cudgel by Trumpites in their battles with some mainstream news organizations, "fake news" — that is, political satire packaged as information — was the province of Jon Stewart-quoting progressives at the peak of the George W. Bush years. To many in 2004, searing dispatches from "The Daily Show" (which billed itself as "the most trusted name in fake news") and The Onion seemed like the best weapon against Washington spin and obfuscation. (Immediately after Mr. Bush's re-election in 2004, for example, The Onion published an article titled "Nation's Poor Win Election for Nation's Rich.")

A most insincere form of flattery: In 2004, fake news had become the "the comic trope of the moment," the Times article's author, Warren St. John, wrote. Much of that could be chalked up to the rising cultural influence of "The Daily Show," which had become something of a mirror-image Fox News for urban ironists ever since Mr. Stewart took over from Craig Kilborn as the host in 1999. (Stephen Colbert, a star correspondent, would push the envelope even further a year after the article was published, creating a fake news show, "The Colbert Report," starring a fake newsman alter ego.)

This was also a peak era of influence for The Onion, which by 2004 had become a must-read for the president's critics as it expanded its

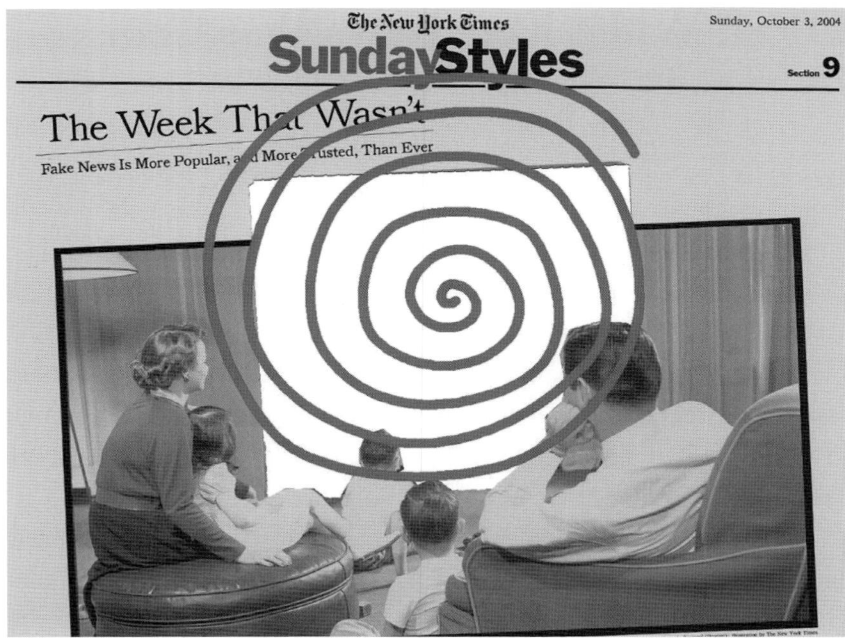

The New York Times

Sunday, October 3, 2004

SundayStyles

Section 9

The Week That Wasn't

Fake News Is More Popular, and More Trusted, Than Ever

THE NEW YORK TIMES

print edition to new cities. Other humorists, including Sacha Baron Cohen and Andy Borowitz, were also mining the faux-news format for laughs. Even mainstream organizations were dipping a toe. Episodes of ABC's "Prime Time Live" closed with a musical rendition of satirical headlines. CNN's "Larry King Live" hired the comedian Mo Rocca as a wisecracking correspondent at political conventions.

The big picture: Much like the present political moment, there was no shortage of political rage in 2004. Democrats still felt cheated in the wake of the hanging chads of the 2000 election, and the Iraq War had turned into a bloody quagmire. In this atmosphere of simmering resentment, satirical news provided a release, as well as mass-market means for those who felt alienated by Bush-era policies to tweak the powers that be. This was also the last era before the internet and social media splintered American news consumption habits, meaning there was still a recognizable institutional news voice that made sense to parody.

You know, for kids: The government was hardly the only target. By lampooning the staid, self-important tone of some traditional news broadcasts, satirists sought to upset legacy media conventions. "There's some weird handcuffs on the mainstream news so that they feel that no matter what, they have to present both sides of the argument, even if one side of an argument is wrong," said Ben Karlin, executive producer of "The Daily Show," in the Times article.

To many, joke news reports provided an alternative context for news controversies like John Kerry's Swift boat kerfuffle. The down-is-up logic of satirical news found a home with the ever-alienated members of Generation X, who had come of age watching Weekend Update on "Saturday Night Live" and National Lampoon's news parodies.

Millennials, too, were just joining the audience, armed with their much-noted distrust of large institutions. Many seemed to agree with the old saying that "a joke is truth wrapped in a smile." The Times article cited a study by Pew Research Center showing that 21 percent of people under 30 said they were learning their news about the 2004 presidential campaign from satirical sources like "The Daily Show," up from 9 percent in 2000.

Fake news as old news? Eventually, the fake news media would face the same headwinds as the real news media. In 2013, after a period of declining advertising revenues, The Onion ceased publication of its 25-year-old print edition. It turned to new, digital targets instead: ClickHole, its parody of click-bait news aggregators, and "A Very Fatal Murder," a parody of "Serial"-style true crime podcasts.

And, as with any revolution (the Soviets, the punks), the rebels eventually became the establishment. Mr. Stewart went on to host the Oscars. Steve Carell became a sitcom star. But nothing went more establishment than the term itself. In January, President Trump himself hosted his own form of the Oscars: the Fake News Awards, an anti-media project meant to tar news reports that he believed were unfair to him.

CHAPTER 2

Facebook, and How Fake News Spreads

At the end of 2017, Facebook reported having 1.4 billion active daily users. For many users, Facebook is the default platform for sharing and reading breaking stories. Facebook is also an advertising platform. For a price almost anyone can target readers using criteria based on age, interests and keywords. Could Facebook's platform to be used to "nudge" enough voters to change the outcome of an election? Does social media do more harm to society than good when it comes to establishing truth and encouraging meaningful dialogue? These are increasingly urgent questions.

Facebook and the Digital Virus Called Fake News

OPINION | BY THE NEW YORK TIMES | NOV. 19, 2016

THIS YEAR, THE ADAGE that "falsehood flies and the truth comes limping after it" doesn't begin to describe the problem. That idea assumes that the truth eventually catches up. There's not much evidence of this happening for the millions of people taken in by the fake news stories — like Pope Francis endorsing Donald Trump or Mr. Trump pulling ahead of Hillary Clinton in the popular vote — that have spread on social media sites.

Most of the fake news stories are produced by scammers looking to make a quick buck. The vast majority of them take far-right positions. But a big part of the responsibility for this scourge rests with internet companies like Facebook and Google, which have made it possible for fake news to be shared nearly instantly with millions of users and have been slow to block it from their sites.

Mark Zuckerberg, the founder and chief executive of Facebook, has dismissed the notion that fake news is prevalent on his platform or that it had an influence on the election. But according to a BuzzFeed News analysis, during the last three months of the presidential campaign, the 20 top fake news stories on Facebook generated more engagement — shares, likes and comments — than the 20 top stories from real news websites.

These hoaxes are not just bouncing around among like-minded conspiracy theorists; candidates and elected officials are sharing them, too. Senator Ben Sasse, Republican of Nebraska, on Thursday tweeted about people who have been paid to riot against Mr. Trump — an idea propagated by fake news stories. A man who wrote a number of false news reports told The Washington Post that Trump supporters and campaign officials often shared his false anti-Clinton posts without bothering to confirm the facts and that he believes his work may have helped elect the Republican nominee.

Abroad, the dissemination of fake news on Facebook, which reaches 1.8 billion people globally, has been a longstanding problem. In countries like Myanmar, deceptive internet content has reportedly contributed to ethnic violence. And it has influenced elections in Indonesia, the Philippines and elsewhere. Social media sites have also been used to spread misinformation about the referendum on the peace deal in Colombia and about Ebola in West Africa.

Facebook says it is working on weeding out such fabrications. It said last Monday that it would no longer place Facebook-powered ads on fake news websites, a move that could cost Facebook and those fake news sites a lucrative source of revenue. Earlier on the same day, Google said it would stop letting those sites use its ad placement network. These steps would help, but Facebook, in particular, owes its users, and democracy itself, far more.

Facebook has demonstrated that it can effectively block content like click-bait articles and spam from its platform by tweaking its algorithms, which determine what links, photos and ads users see in their news feeds. Nobody outside the company knows exactly how its software works and why you might see posts shared by some of your friends frequently and others rarely. Recently, the company acknowledged that it had allowed businesses to target or exclude users for ads for housing, employment and credit based on their ethnicity, in apparent violation of anti-discrimination laws. It has said it will stop that practice.

Facebook managers are constantly changing and refining the algorithms, which means the system is malleable and subject to human judgment. This summer, Facebook decided to show more posts from friends and family members in users' news feeds and reduce stories from news organizations, because that's what it said users wanted. If it can do that, surely its programmers can train the software to spot bogus stories and outwit the people producing this garbage.

Blocking misinformation will help protect the company's brand and credibility. Some platforms have suffered when they have failed to address users' concerns. Twitter users, for instance, have backed away from that platform because of abusive trolling, threatening posts and hate speech, which the company hasn't been able to control.

Mr. Zuckerberg himself has spoken at length about how social media can help improve society. In a 2012 letter to investors, he said it could "bring a more honest and transparent dialogue around government that could lead to more direct empowerment of people, more accountability for officials and better solutions to some of the biggest problems of our time."

None of that will happen if he continues to let liars and con artists hijack his platform.

To Stir Discord in 2016, Russians Turned Most Often to Facebook

BY SHEERA FRENKEL AND KATIE BENNER | FEB. 17, 2018

SAN FRANCISCO — In 2014, Russians working for a shadowy firm called the Internet Research Agency started gathering American followers in online groups focused on issues like religion and immigration. Around mid-2015, the Russians began buying digital ads to spread their messages. A year later, they tapped their followers to help organize political rallies across the United States.

Their digital instrument of choice for all of these actions? Facebook and its photo-sharing site Instagram.

The social network, more than any other technology tool, was singled out on Friday by the Justice Department when prosecutors charged 13 Russians and three companies for executing a scheme to subvert the 2016 election and support Donald J. Trump's presidential campaign. In a 37-page indictment, officials detailed how the Russians repeatedly turned to Facebook and Instagram, often using stolen identities to pose as Americans, to sow discord among the electorate by creating Facebook groups, distributing divisive ads and posting inflammatory images.

While the indictment does not accuse Facebook of any wrongdoing, it provided the first comprehensive account from the authorities of how critical the company's platforms had been to the Russian campaign to disrupt the 2016 election. Facebook and Instagram were mentioned 41 times, while other technology that the Russians used was featured far less. Twitter was referred to nine times, YouTube once and the electronic payments company PayPal 11 times.

It is unprecedented for an American technology company to be so central to what the authorities say was a foreign scheme to commit election fraud in the United States. The indictment further batters Facebook's image after it has spent months grappling with questions about how it was misused and why it did not act earlier to prevent that activity.

Jonathan Albright, research director at Columbia University's Tow Center for Digital Journalism, said the indictment laid bare how effectively Facebook could be turned against the country.

"Facebook built incredibly effective tools which let Russia profile citizens here in the U.S. and figure out how to manipulate us," Mr. Albright said. "Facebook, essentially, gave them everything they needed." He added that many of the tools that the Russians used, including those that allow ads to be targeted and that show how widespread an ad becomes, still pervade Facebook.

Facebook, with more than two billion members on the social network alone, has long struggled with what its sites show and the kind of illicit activity it may enable, from selling unlicensed guns to broadcasting live killings. The company's business depends on people being highly engaged with what is posted on its sites, which in turn helps make it a marquee destination for advertisers.

When suggestions first arose after the 2016 election that Facebook may have influenced the outcome, Mark Zuckerberg, the company's chief executive, dismissed the concerns. But by last September, Facebook had disclosed that the Internet Research Agency had bought divisive ads on hot-button issues through the company. It later said 150 million Americans had seen the Russian propaganda on the social network and Instagram.

The resulting firestorm has damaged Facebook's reputation. Company officials, along with executives from Google and YouTube, were grilled by lawmakers last fall. Facebook has since hired thousands of people to help monitor content and has worked with Robert S. Mueller III, the special counsel leading the investigation into Russian election interference. It has also changed its advertising policy so that any ad that mentions a candidate's name goes through a more stringent vetting process. Mr. Zuckerberg has vowed to not let Facebook be abused by bad actors.

Yet Facebook's multiple mentions in Friday's indictment renew questions of why the world's biggest social media company didn't catch the Russian activity earlier or do more to stop it. How effective the company's new efforts to reduce foreign manipulation have been is also unclear.

Rob Goldman, Facebook's vice president of advertising, waded into the discussion on Friday with a series of tweets that argued that Russia's goal was to sow chaos among the electorate rather than to force a certain outcome in the election. On Saturday, President Trump cited those tweets as evidence that Russia's disinformation campaign was not aimed at handing him a victory.

In Silicon Valley, where Facebook has its headquarters, some critics pilloried the company after the indictment became public.

"Mueller's indictment underscores the central role of Facebook and other platforms in the Russian interference in 2016," said Roger McNamee, a Silicon Valley venture capitalist who had invested early in Facebook. "In its heyday, television brought the country together, giving viewers a shared set of facts and experiences. Facebook does just the opposite, enabling every user to have a unique set of facts, driving the country apart for profit."

Joel Kaplan, Facebook's vice president of global policy, said in a statement that the company was grateful the government was taking action "against those who abused our service and exploited the openness of our democratic process."

He added that Facebook was working with the Federal Bureau of Investigation ahead of this year's midterm elections to ensure that a similar manipulation campaign would not take place. "We know we have more to do to prevent against future attacks," he said.

Facebook has previously questioned whether law enforcement should be more involved in helping to stop the threat from nation state actors. Facebook said it worked closely with the special counsel's investigation.

YouTube did not respond to a request for comment, while Twitter declined to comment. PayPal said in a statement that it has worked closely with law enforcement and "is intensely focused on combating and preventing the illicit use of our services."

According to the indictment, the Internet Research Agency, created in 2014 in St. Petersburg and employing about 80 people, was given the job of interfering with elections and political processes.

The group began using American social media to achieve those aims in 2014, when it started making Facebook pages dedicated to social issues like race and religion. Over the next two years, the indictment said, the Russians stole the identities of real Americans to create fake personas and fake accounts on social media. The group then used those to populate and promote Facebook pages like United Muslims of America, Blacktivist and Secured Borders.

By 2016, the indictment said, the size of some of these Russian-controlled Facebook groups had ballooned to hundreds of thousands of followers.

The Russians then used these groups to push various messages, including telling Americans not to vote in the 2016 election for either Mr. Trump or his opponent, Hillary Clinton. In October 2016, according to the indictment, one Russian-controlled Instagram account called Woke Blacks posted a message saying: "Hatred for Trump is misleading the people and forcing Blacks to vote Killary. We cannot resort to the lesser of two devils. Then we'd surely be better off without voting AT ALL."

Around 2015, according to the indictment, the Russians also started purchasing ads on Facebook and other social media sites like Twitter, targeting specific communities within the United States. The group used stolen PayPal accounts to pay for the ads and to promote posts, spending hundreds of thousands of dollars on the outreach.

In one ad, published to promote a Facebook event called "Down with Hillary," an image of Mrs. Clinton was shown with a black "X" painted across her face. The text read, "Hillary Clinton is the co-author of Obama's anti-police and anti-Constitutional propaganda."

By mid-2016, according to the indictment, the Russians were using their fake Facebook personas to organize political rallies in the United States. That June, for example, posing as the United Muslims of America on Facebook, they promoted a rally called "Support Hillary. Save American Muslims." For an August 2016 event organized through Facebook, the Russians also paid for a cage to be built that was large enough to hold an actress depicting Mrs. Clinton in a prison uniform.

At every step, the Russians used Facebook's own tools to make sure their propaganda was as effective as possible. Those tools allowed them to get real-time results on which types of ad campaigns were reaching their target audience or which posts were getting the most engagement with viewers.

Researchers said that those tools are still widely available and that while the company has worked to remove fake accounts and stem the flow of disinformation, it has refused to let outside researchers examine the data on how Russian actors used the platform so effectively.

"They're taking steps to fix this, but there's no easy solution," Anton Vuljaj, a Republican media strategist who has advised campaigns and media groups, said of Facebook and other social media companies. "This also shows that the public needs to be more vigilant about what is real and what is not online."

Facebook Is Ignoring Anti-Abortion Fake News

BY ROSSALYN WARREN | NOV. 10, 2017

LAST YEAR, JUST WEEKS BEFORE the election, an article from a site called Mad World News began circulating around Facebook. The headline read "Before Applauding Hillary's Abortion Remarks, Know the One Fact She Ignored."

In the article, the writer says she wants to expose Hillary Clinton's lies about late-term abortions. She argues that a baby never needs to be aborted to save a mother's life but doesn't cite any sources or studies, and presents anecdotes and opinion as fact. Midway through the story, she shares an illustration of what she calls a "Partial-Birth Procedure" — a procedure banned in the United States. In it, she describes how a doctor "jams scissors into the baby's skull" and how "the child's brains are sucked out."

ERIC THAYER FOR THE NEW YORK TIMES

Colin Stretch, general counsel for Facebook, testifying on Capitol Hill last week.

"Don't let these lies kill another child in such a horrific manner," she says, concluding the piece. The article was engaged with at least 1.1 million times, making it the most-shared article about abortion on Facebook last year, according to BuzzSumo, a company that tracks social sharing.

Last week, the company's general counsel appeared before Congress alongside his counterparts from Twitter and Google to testify on the company's role in distributing misinformation ahead of the 2016 presidential election. Facebook says it's taking "fake news" seriously. It has a label for "disputed" stories, brought in independent fact-checking partners and allows users to report false articles.

It's not clear whether these attempts to tackle misinformation will work; critics have called them ineffective and slow. But there's another problem, too. So far, Facebook and the public have focused almost solely on politics and Russian interference in the United States election. What they haven't addressed is the vast amount of misinformation and unevidenced stories about reproductive rights, science and health.

Evidence-based, credible articles about abortion from reputable news outlets like The New York Times and The Washington Post didn't make it to the top of the list of "most shared" articles on Facebook last year, according to BuzzSumo. But articles from the site LifeNews.com did.

LifeNews, which has just under one million followers on Facebook, is one of several large anti-abortion sites that can command hundreds of thousands of views on a single post. These sites produce vast amounts of misinformation; the Facebook page for the organization Live Action, for instance, has two million Facebook followers and posts videos claiming there's a correlation between abortion and breast cancer. And their stories often generate more engagement than the content produced by mainstream news organizations, said Sharon Kann, the program director for abortion rights and reproductive health at Media Matters, a watchdog group. People on Facebook engage with anti-abortion content more than abortion-rights content at a "disproportionate rate," she said, which, as a result of the company's algorithms, means more people see it.

Facebook's current initiatives to crack down on fake news can, theoretically, be applicable to misinformation on other issues. However, there are several human and technical barriers that prevent misinformation about reproductive rights from being identified, checked and removed at the same — already slow — rate as other misleading stories.

First, the question of what's considered a "fake news" site is not always black and white. Facebook says it has been tackling the sources of fake news by eliminating the ability to "spoof" domains and by deleting Facebook pages linked to spam activity. For example, this year Facebook identified and deleted more than 30 pages owned by Macedonian publishers, who used them to push out fake stories about United States politics, after alarms had been sounded about sites in the country spreading misinformation about the 2016 campaign. (Facebook says some of the sites may have been taken down for other terms-of-service violations.) But anti-abortion sites are different. They do not mimic real publications, and they publish pieces on real events alongside factually incorrect or thinly sourced stories, which helps blur the line between what's considered a news blog and "fake news."

Second, Facebook says one of its key aims in tackling fake news is to remove the profit incentive, because it says "most false news is financially motivated." It says it hopes to do that by making it more difficult for the people behind the fake news sites to buy ads on its platform and by detecting and deleting spam accounts, which it says are a major force behind the spread of misinformation.

However, the incentive for the people who write content for anti-abortion news sites and Facebook pages is ideological, not financial. Anti-abortion, anti-science content isn't being written by spammers hoping to make money, but by ordinary people who are driven by religious or political beliefs. Their aim isn't to profit from ads. It's to convince readers of their viewpoint: that abortion is morally wrong, that autism is caused by vaccines or that climate change isn't real.

Finally, public pressure influences where Facebook directs its attention. Facebook may be focused on fake news and the United States election now, but its efforts to prevent the spread of misinformation in the buildup to the election were practically nonexistent. It took action only after intense scrutiny.

Now Facebook and its fact-checking partners say its focus is "on the worst of the worst, on the clear hoaxes spread by spammers for their own gain." Simply put, without increased pressure, Facebook's technical efforts and its human efforts, like fact-checkers' trawling through flagged content, make it likely that the company, in the months to come, will be seeking out only the "obvious" flags of fake news stories and not the misinformation that is fueled by real people with no financial incentive. That is why those of us who are concerned by the misinformation around reproductive rights need to make ourselves heard.

The Irish government says it will hold a referendum next year on whether to relax the country's strict ban on abortion. Some abortion-rights campaigners have expressed concern over the role of misinformation on social media platforms like Facebook in the lead-up to the vote, but it's far from clear whether those concerns are being listened to.

Curbing the spread of fake news is no easy task, and Facebook says it cannot "become arbiters of truth" in the fight against fake news. But at the very least, the company can address its continuing role in inadvertently spreading false information about issues that go beyond the United States election and Russia.

Facebook's Problem Isn't Fake News — It's the Rest of the Internet

BY JOHN HERRMAN | DEC. 22, 2016

LAST THURSDAY, after weeks of criticism over its role in the proliferation of falsehoods and propaganda during the presidential election, Facebook announced its plan to combat "hoaxes" and "fake news." The company promised to test new tools that would allow users to report misinformation, and to enlist fact-checking organizations including Snopes and PolitiFact to help litigate the veracity of links reported as suspect. By analyzing patterns of reading and sharing, the company said, it might be able to penalize articles that are shared at especially low rates by those who read them — a signal of dissatisfaction. Finally, it said, it would try to put economic pressure on bad actors in three ways: by banning disputed stories from its advertising ecosystem; by making it harder to impersonate credible sites on the platform; and, crucially, by penalizing websites that are loaded with too many ads.

Over the past month the colloquial definition of "fake news" has expanded beyond usefulness, implicating everything from partisan news to satire to conspiracy theories before being turned, finally, back against its creators. Facebook's fixes address a far more narrow definition. "We've focused our efforts on the worst of the worst, on the clear hoaxes spread by spammers for their own gain," wrote Adam Mosseri, a vice president for news feed, in a blog post.

Facebook's political news ecosystem during the 2016 election was vast and varied. There was, of course, content created by outside news media that was shared by users, but there were also reams of content — posts, images, videos — created on Facebook-only pages, and still more media created by politicians themselves. During the election, it was apparent to almost anyone with an account that Facebook was teeming with political content, much of it extremely partisan or pitched, its sourcing sometimes obvious, other times obscured, and often simply beside the point — memes or rants or theories that spoke for themselves.

Facebook seems to have zeroed in on only one component of this ecosystem — outside websites — and within it, narrow types of bad actors. These firms are, generally speaking, paid by advertising companies independent of Facebook, which are unaware of or indifferent to their partners' sources of audience. Accordingly, Facebook's anti-hoax measures seek to regulate these sites by punishing them not just for what they do on Facebook, but for what they do outside of it.

"We've found that a lot of fake news is financially motivated," Mosseri wrote. "Spammers make money by masquerading as well-known news organizations and posting hoaxes that get people to visit to their sites, which are often mostly ads." The proposed solution: "Analyzing publisher sites to detect where policy enforcement actions might be necessary."

The stated targets of Facebook's efforts are precisely defined, but its formulation of the problem implicates, to a lesser degree, much more than just "the worst of the worst." Consider this characterization of what makes a "fake news" site a bad platform citizen: It uses Facebook to capture receptive audiences by spreading lies and then converts those audiences into money by borrowing them from Facebook, luring them to an outside site larded with obnoxious ads. The site's sin of fabrication is made worse by its profit motive, which is cast here as a sort of arbitrage scheme. But an acceptable news site does more or less the same thing: It uses Facebook to capture receptive audiences by spreading not-lies and then converts those audiences into money by luring them to an outside site not-quite larded with not-as-obnoxious ads. In either case, Facebook users are being taken out of the safe confines of the platform into areas that Facebook does not and cannot control.

In this context, this "fake news" problem reads less as a distinct new phenomenon than as a flaring symptom of an older, more existential anxiety that Facebook has been grappling with for years: its continued (albeit diminishing) dependence on the same outside web that it, and other platforms, have begun to replace. Facebook's plan for "fake news" is no doubt intended to curb certain types of misinformation. But it's also a continuation of the company's bigger and more consequential project — to capture the experiences of the web it wants and from which it can profit, but to insulate itself from the parts that it doesn't and can't. This may help solve a problem within the ecosystem of outside publishers — an ecosystem that, in the distribution machinery of Facebook, is becoming redundant, and perhaps even obsolete.

As Facebook has grown, so have its ambitions. Its mantralike mission (to "connect the world") is rivaled among internet companies perhaps by only that of Google (to "organize the world's information") in terms of sheer scope. In the run-up to Facebook's initial public offering, Mark Zuckerberg told investors that the company makes decisions "not optimizing for what's going to happen in the next year, but to set us up to really be in this world where every product experience you have is social, and that's all powered by Facebook."

To understand what such ambition looks like in practice, consider Facebook's history. It started as an inward-facing website, closed off from both the web around it and the general public. It was a place to connect with other people, and where content was created primarily by other users: photos, wall posts, messages. This system quickly grew larger and more complex, leading to the creation, in 2006, of the news feed — a single location in which users could find updates from all of their Facebook friends, in roughly reverse-chronological order.

When the news feed was announced, before the emergence of the modern Facebook sharing ecosystem, Facebook's operating definition of "news" was pointedly friend-centric. "Now, whenever you log in, you'll get the latest headlines generated by the activity of your friends and social groups," the announcement about the news feed said. This would soon change.

In the ensuing years, as more people spent more time on Facebook, and following the addition of "Like" and "Share" functions within Facebook, the news feed grew into a personalized portal not just for personal updates but also for the cornucopia of media that existed elsewhere online: links to videos, blog posts, games and more or less anything else published on an external website, including news articles. This potent mixture accelerated Facebook's change from a place for keeping up with family and friends to a place for keeping up, additionally, with the web in general, as curated by your friends and family. Facebook's purview continued to widen as its user base grew and then acquired their first smartphones; its app became an essential lens through which hundreds of millions of people interacted with one another, with the rest of the web and, increasingly, with the world at large.

Facebook, in other words, had become an interface for the whole web rather than just one more citizen of it. By sorting and mediating the internet, Facebook inevitably began to change it. In the previous decade, the popularity of Google influenced how websites worked, in noticeable ways: Titles and headlines were written in search-friendly formats; pages or articles would be published not just to cover the news but, more specifically, to address Google searchers' queries about the news, the canonical example being The Huffington Post's famous "What Time Does The Super Bowl Start?" Publishers built entire business models around attracting search traffic, and search-engine optimization, S.E.O., became an industry unto itself. Facebook's influence on the web — and in particular, on news publishers — was similarly profound. Publishers began taking into consideration how their headlines, and stories, might travel within Facebook. Some embraced the site as a primary source of visitors; some pursued this strategy into absurdity and exploitation.

Facebook, for its part, paid close attention to the sorts of external content people were sharing on its platform and to the techniques used by websites to get an edge. It adapted continually. It provided greater video functionality, reducing the need to link to outside videos or embed them from YouTube. As people began posting more news, it created previews for links, with larger images and headlines and longer summaries; eventually, it created Instant Articles, allowing certain publishers (including The Times) to publish stories natively in Facebook. At the same time, it routinely sought to penalize sites it judged to be using the platform in bad faith, taking aim at "clickbait," an older cousin of "fake news," with a series of design and algorithm updates. As Facebook's influence over online media became unavoidably obvious, its broad approach to users and the web became clearer: If the network became a popular venue for a certain sort of content or behavior, the company generally and reasonably tried to make that behavior easier or that content more accessible. This tended to mean, however, bringing it in-house.

To Facebook, the problem with "fake news" is not just the obvious damage to the discourse, but also with the harm it inflicts upon the platform. People sharing hoax stories were, presumably, happy enough with what they were seeing. But the people who would then encounter those stories in their feeds were subjected to a less positive experience. They were sent outside the platform to a website where they realized they were being deceived, or where they were exposed to ads or something that felt like spam, or where they were persuaded to share something that might later make them look like a rube. These users might rightly associate these experiences not just with their friends on the platform, or with the sites peddling the bogus stories but also with the platform itself. This created, finally, an obvious issue for a company built on attention, advertising and the promotion of outside brands. From the platform's perspective, "fake news" is essentially a user-experience problem resulting from a lingering design issue — akin to slow-loading news websites that feature auto-playing videos and obtrusive ads.

Increasingly, legitimacy within Facebook's ecosystem is conferred according to a participant's relationship to the platform's design. A verified user telling a lie, be it a friend from high school or the president elect, isn't breaking the rules; he is, as his checkmark suggests, who he represents himself to be. A post making false claims about a product is Facebook's problem only if that post is labeled an ad. A user video promoting a conspiracy theory becomes a problem only when it leads to the violation of community guidelines against, for example, user harassment. Facebook contains a lot more than just news, including a great deal of content that is newslike, partisan, widely shared and often misleading. Content that has been, and will be, immune from current "fake news" critiques and crackdowns, because it never had the opportunity to declare itself news in the first place. To publish lies as "news" is to break a promise; to publish lies as "content" is not.

That the "fake news" problem and its proposed solutions have been defined by Facebook as link issues — as a web issue — aligns nicely with a longer-term future in which Facebook's interface with the web is diminished. Indeed, it heralds the coming moment when posts from outside are suspect by default: out of place, inefficient, little better than spam.

JOHN HERRMAN IS A DAVID CARR FELLOW AT THE NEW YORK TIMES.

Facebook Mounts Effort to Limit Tide of Fake News

BY MIKE ISAAC | DEC. 15, 2016

FOR WEEKS, Facebook has been questioned about its role in spreading fake news. Now the company has mounted its most concerted effort to combat the problem.

Facebook said on Thursday that it had begun a series of experiments to limit misinformation on its site. The tests include making it easier for its 1.8 billion members to report fake news, and creating partnerships with outside fact-checking organizations to help it indicate when articles are false. The company is also changing some advertising practices to stop purveyors of fake news from profiting from it.

Facebook, the social network, is in a tricky position with these tests. It has long regarded itself as a neutral place where people can freely post, read and view content, and it has said it does not want to be an arbiter of truth. But as its reach and influence have grown, it has had to confront questions about its moral obligations and ethical standards regarding what appears on the network.

Its experiments on curtailing fake news show that Facebook recognizes it has a deepening responsibility for what is on its site. But Facebook also must tread cautiously in making changes, because it is wary of exposing itself to claims of censorship.

"We really value giving people a voice, but we also believe we need to take responsibility for the spread of fake news on our platform," said Adam Mosseri, a Facebook vice president who is in charge of its news feed, the company's method of distributing information to its global audience.

He said the changes — which, if successful, may be available to a wide audience — resulted from many months of internal discussion about how to handle false news articles shared on the network.

What impact Facebook's moves will have on fake news is unclear. The issue is not confined to the social network, with a vast ecosystem of false news creators who thrive on online advertising and who can use other social media and search engines to propagate their work. Google, Twitter and message boards like 4chan and Reddit have all been criticized for being part of that chain.

Still, Facebook has taken the most heat over fake news. The company has been under that spotlight since Nov. 8, when Donald J. Trump was elected the 45th president. Mr. Trump's unexpected victory almost immediately led people to focus on whether Facebook had influenced the electorate, especially with the rise of hyperpartisan sites on the network and many examples of misinformation, such as a false article that claimed Pope Francis had endorsed Mr. Trump for president that was shared nearly a million times across the site.

Mark Zuckerberg, Facebook's chief executive, has said he did not believe that the social network had influenced the election result, calling it "a pretty crazy idea." Yet the intense scrutiny of the company on the issue has caused internal divisions and has pushed Mr. Zuckerberg to say he was trying to find ways to reduce the problem.

In an interview, Mr. Mosseri said Facebook did not think its news feed had directly caused people to vote for a particular candidate, given that "the magnitude of fake news across Facebook is one fraction of a percent of the content across the network."

Facebook has changed the way its news feed works before. In August, the company announced changes to marginalize what it considered "clickbait," the sensational headlines that rarely live up to their promise. This year, Facebook also gave priority to content shared by friends and family, a move that shook some publishers that rely on the social network for much of their traffic. The company is also constantly fine-tuning its algorithms to serve what its users most want to see, an effort to keep its audience returning regularly.

This time, Facebook is making it easier to flag content that may be fake. Users can report a post they dislike in their feed, but when Facebook asks for a reason, the site presents them with a list of limited and vague options, including the cryptic "I don't think it should be on

Facebook." In Facebook's new experiment, users will have a choice to flag the post as fake news and have the option to message the friend who originally shared the piece to tell him or her the article is false.

If an article receives enough flags as fake, it can be directed to a coalition of groups that will fact-check it. The groups include Snopes, PolitiFact, The Associated Press, FactCheck.org and ABC News. They will check the article and can mark it as a "disputed" piece, a designation that will be seen on Facebook.

Partner organizations will not be paid, the companies said. Some characterized the fact-checking as an extension of their journalistic efforts.

"We actually regard this as a big part of our core mission," James Goldston, the president of ABC News, said in an interview. "If that core mission isn't helping people regard the real from the fake news, I don't know what our mission is."

Disputed articles will ultimately appear lower in the news feed. If users still decide to share such an article, they will receive a pop-up reminding them that the accuracy of the piece is in question.

Facebook said it was casting a wide net to add more partners to its fact-checking coalition and may move outside of the United States with the initiative if early experiments go well. The company is also part of the First Draft Coalition, an effort with other technology and media companies including Twitter, Google, The New York Times and CNN, to combat the spread of fake news online.

In another change in how the news feed works, articles that many users read but do not share will be ranked lower on people's feeds. Mr. Mosseri said a low ratio of sharing an article after it has been read could be perceived as a negative signal, one that might reflect that the article was misleading or of poor quality.

"Facebook was inevitably going to have to curate the platform much more carefully, and this seems like a reasonably transparent method of intervention," said Emily Bell, director at the Tow Center for Digital Journalism at Columbia University.

"But the fake cat is already out of the imaginary bag," Ms. Bell added. "If they didn't try and do something about it, next time around it could have far worse consequences."

Facebook also plans to impede the economics of spreading fake articles across the network. Fake news purveyors generally make money when people click on the false articles and are directed to third-party websites, the majority of which are filled with dozens of low-cost ads.

Facebook will review those third-party links and check for things like whether the page is mostly filled with advertising content — a dead giveaway for spam sites — or to see whether a link masquerades as a different site, like a fake version of The New York Times. Such sites would not be eligible to display Facebook advertising on their pages.

Articles disputed by the fact-checking coalition will also not be eligible to be inserted into Facebook ads, a tactic viral spammers have used to spread fake news quickly and gain more clicks on their websites.

Facebook said that in these early experiments it would deal with only fake news content; it does not plan to flag opinion posts or other content that could not be easily classified. The changes will not affect satirical sites like The Onion, which often jabs at political subjects through tongue-in-cheek humor.

Facebook must take something else into consideration: its profit. Any action taken to reduce popular content, even if it is fake news, could hurt the company's priority of keeping its users engaged on the platform. People spend an average of more than 50 minutes a day on Facebook, and the company wants that number to grow.

Executives at Facebook stressed the overriding factor right now is not just engagement.

"I think of Facebook as a technology company, but I recognize we have a greater responsibility than just building technology that information flows through," Mr. Zuckerberg wrote in a post on Thursday. "We have a responsibility to make sure Facebook has the greatest positive impact on the world."

Facebook to Let Users Rank Credibility of News

BY SHEERA FRENKEL AND SAPNA MAHESHWARI | JAN. 19, 2018

SAN FRANCISCO — Facebook said on Friday that it planned to prioritize high-quality news on the social network by allowing its users to rank news sources that they see as the most credible and trustworthy.

The initiative, which follows an overhaul that Facebook announced last week to emphasize posts, videos and photos shared by friends and family, will not increase the amount of news on the social network. But the move has implications for what news will be consumed on Facebook, potentially favoring the most familiar names in media that are seen as the most credible, while tilting away from lesser-known and less-trusted outlets without solving the issue of whether news could still be distorted.

"There's too much sensationalism, misinformation and polarization in the world today," Mark Zuckerberg, Facebook's chief executive, wrote in a post on Friday. "We decided that having the community determine which sources are broadly trusted would be most objective."

The shift is another signal of Facebook's ability — this time using the collective power of its more than two billion members worldwide — to play kingmaker with publishers. Many publishers have long relied on Facebook to reach audiences, and they largely reacted with disappointment last week when the company said it would play down news overall.

The move is also the most recent by Facebook to counter charges that not enough was being done to stamp out fake news and disinformation on its platform. The company was dogged by criticism in late 2016 after the presidential election that too many false stories attacking Hillary Clinton had spread on its site, that way affecting the election's outcome. Last year, Facebook also acknowledged that Russian agents had used the site to spread divisive and polarizing ads and posts.

The same criticism has also engulfed other social media companies such as Twitter, which on Friday said it was emailing notifications to 677,775 people in the United States that they had interacted with Russian propaganda accounts around the time of the 2016 election.

For publishers, Facebook's new ranking system raised immediate concerns, including whether crowdsourcing users' opinions on trustworthiness might be open to manipulation.

"It is absolutely a positive move to start to try to separate the wheat from the chaff in terms of reputation and use brands as proxies for trust," said Jason Kint, the chief executive of Digital Content Next, a trade group that represents entertainment and news organizations, including The New York Times. "But the devil's in the details on how they're going to actually execute on that."

He continued, "How does that get hacked or gamed? How do we trust the ranking system? There's a slew of questions at this point."

The new system could also potentially favor publishers who are partisan. Facebook users, asked to rank which news they most trust, could choose sites that speak most clearly to their personal beliefs, in effect reducing the prominence of publishers who try to maintain an objective tone.

David Kaye, the United Nations' Special Rapporteur on freedom of expression, said that Facebook would probably face more difficult questions as it rolled out the new ranking program globally.

"What will happen in situations where a community determines that a news source is trustworthy, but that news source is censored, or illegal, in that country?" asked Mr. Kaye, noting that in many parts of the world, governments controlled all official news channels while independent news sources were outlawed or forced to publish pseudo-anonymously.

In the past, he added, Facebook has abided by local rules where it operates abroad.

"What will Mark Zuckerberg do when the needs of the community, in what it determines is trusted news, are different from what the government determines? Who will Facebook side with?" said Mr. Kaye.

Raju Narisetti, the chief executive of the Gizmodo Media Group, the unit of Univision that operates Jezebel and other sites, said there was a "great irony" that Facebook, which has traditionally left decisions up to an algorithm that incorporates the behaviors of its members, would open the decision-making to its users on such a matter. He added that the user-generated ranking system "is a massive abdication of its social responsibility, as a vital platform, to be a good custodian of the Fourth Estate globally."

Other experiments that Facebook has tried with news in the past have sometimes gone awry or had unintended consequences. For example, a recent test to remove all news publishers from the News Feed and to place them under a separate tab in six countries, including Bolivia and Slovakia, yielded an unexpected result of magnifying the amount of fake news on the platform.

In his post on Friday, Mr. Zuckerberg said the newest change "will only shift the balance of news you see towards sources that are determined to be trusted by the community."

Facebook said news would be prioritized according to the new ranking system starting Monday, before expanding globally. Some Facebook users have already been asked to rank the trustworthiness of news sites which appear on the social network. In one survey, people were asked if they recognized a number of websites and then asked, "How much do you trust each of these domains?" They were able to choose from a range of answers, including entirely, a lot, somewhat, barely and not at all.

The Silicon Valley company said it would continue polling users to refine and select which news outlets garnered the most trust. It declined to say how many people were polled or which news outlets they were asked about.

"As part of our ongoing quality surveys, we asked a diverse and representative sample of Facebook users across the U.S. to gauge their familiarity with, and trust in, sources of news," said Todd Breasseale, a Facebook spokesman. "We boost links from sources with high trust scores and demote links from sources with low trust scores."

Mr. Zuckerberg has been moving Facebook toward taking more responsibility for what shows up on the social network, especially after the criticism over the 2016 election and the interference by Russian agents. Earlier this month, he described his 2018 goals as including "making sure that time spent on Facebook is time well spent."

In Friday's post, he hinted that ranking the credibility of news sources was just one step, with more potential changes to come.

"I've asked our product teams to make sure we prioritize news that is trustworthy, informative, and local," he wrote. "And we're starting next week with trusted sources."

In Some Countries, Facebook's Fiddling Has Magnified Fake News

BY SHEERA FRENKEL, NICHOLAS CASEY AND PAUL MOZUR | JAN. 14, 2018

SAN FRANCISCO — One morning in October, the editors of Página Siete, Bolivia's third-largest news site, noticed that traffic to their outlet coming from Facebook was plummeting.

The publication had recently been hit by cyberattacks, and editors feared it was being targeted by hackers loyal to the government of President Evo Morales.

But it wasn't the government's fault. It was Facebook's. The Silicon Valley company was testing a new version of its hugely popular News Feed, peeling off professional news sites from what people normally see and relegating them to a new section of Facebook called Explore.

GONZALO PARDO FOR THE NEW YORK TIMES

The newsroom of Página Siete, a Bolivian newspaper. Traffic to the publication's website plunged by 20 percent after Facebook began testing a new version of its News Feed in Bolivia.

Like it or not, Bolivia had become a guinea pig in the company's continual quest to reinvent itself.

As Facebook updates and tweaks its service in order to keep users glued to their screens, countries like Bolivia are ideal testing grounds thanks to their growing, internet-savvy populations. But these changes can have significant consequences, like limiting the audience for non-governmental news sources and — surprisingly — amplifying the impact of fabricated and sensational stories. On Thursday, Facebook announced plans to make similar changes to its News Feed around the world. The company said it was trying to increase "meaningful interaction" on its site by drawing attention to content from family and friends while de-emphasizing content from brands and publishers, including The New York Times.

The changes are being made as the company finds itself embroiled in a larger debate over its role in spreading fake news and misinformation aimed at influencing elections in the United States and other nations.

Facebook said these News Feed modifications were not identical to those introduced last fall in six countries through its Explore program, but both alterations favor posts from friends and family over professional news sites. And what happened in those countries illustrates the unintended consequences of such a change in an online service that now has a global reach of more than two billion people every month.

In Slovakia, where right-wing nationalists took nearly 10 percent of Parliament in 2016, publishers said the changes had actually helped promote fake news. With official news organizations forced to spend money to place themselves in the News Feed, it is now up to users to share information.

"People usually don't share boring news with boring facts," said Filip Struharik, the social media editor of Denník N, a Slovakian subscription news site that saw a 30 percent drop in Facebook engagement after the changes. Mr. Struharik, who has been cataloging the effects of Facebook Explore through a monthly tally, has noted a steady rise in engagement on sites that publish fake or sensationalist news.

A bogus news story that spread in December illustrates the problem, Mr. Struharik said. The story claimed that a Muslim man had thanked a good Samaritan for returning his lost wallet, and had warned the Samaritan of a terrorist attack that was planned at a Christmas market.

The fabricated story circulated so widely that the local police issued a statement saying it wasn't true. But when the police went to issue the warning on Facebook, they found that the message — unlike the fake news story they meant to combat — could no longer appear on News Feed because it came from an official account.

Facebook explained its goals for the Explore program in Slovakia, Sri Lanka, Cambodia, Bolivia, Guatemala and Serbia in a blog post in October. "The goal of this test is to understand if people prefer to have separate places for personal and public content," wrote Adam Mosseri, head of Facebook's News Feed. "There is no current plan to roll this out beyond these test countries."

The company did not respond to a list of questions about the Explore program, but Mr. Mosseri said in a statement on Friday that the company took its role as a "global platform for information" seriously.

"We have a responsibility to the people who read, watch and share news on Facebook, and every test is done with that responsibility in mind," he said.

The impact of the changes to the News Feed were also felt in Cambodia. Months into the experiment (Facebook hasn't said when it will end), Cambodians still don't know where to find trusted, established news on Facebook, said Stuart White, editor of The Phnom Penh Post, an English-language newspaper.

Nongovernmental organizations working on issues like education and health care also complained that the changes broke down lines of communication to Cambodians in need.

Facebook has become particularly important in Cambodia. The country's leader, Hun Sen, has cracked down on political opponents, activists and media, effectively transforming the struggling democracy into a one-party state. Journalists have been arrested, newspapers have been shut down, and Facebook has emerged as an important, more independent channel for information.

That is, if you can find that information. Mr. White recalled a conversation this month with a friend who casually observed the lack of political conversation on Facebook.

"He said he thought the government had banned politics on Facebook," Mr. White said. "He had no idea that Facebook had created Explore or was placing news there. He's a young, urbanite, English-speaking Cambodian. If he didn't know about it, what do you think the effects are on other parts of the country?"

In Bolivia, the alterations to the News Feed also occurred in a country where the government and the press have found themselves at odds, with news sites like Página Siete frequently criticizing Mr. Morales, a left-wing populist who has accumulated enormous power since being elected president in 2006.

"We became the only media to take on the government," said Rodolfo Huallpa, the web editor of Página Siete. Half of the site's traffic came from social media, with the lion's share of that from Facebook, he said. Since Explore was introduced, overall web traffic to the site has dropped 20 percent.

The loss of visitors from Facebook was readily apparent in October, and Mr. Huallpa could communicate with Facebook only through a customer service form letter. He received an automatic reply in return.

After complaints from other outlets, Facebook eventually released a statement on a blog in Spanish explaining the Explore feature and the testing being done in Bolivia and other countries. But Facebook offered no means to contact it, Mr. Huallpa said.

"We can't talk to Zuckerberg, we can't even talk to a customer service representative," said Isabel Mercado, the editor of Página Siete, referring to Facebook's chief executive, Mark Zuckerberg.

The Explore experiment has reduced traffic by 30 to 60 percent at the website of Los Tiempos, the main newspaper of Cochabamba, the

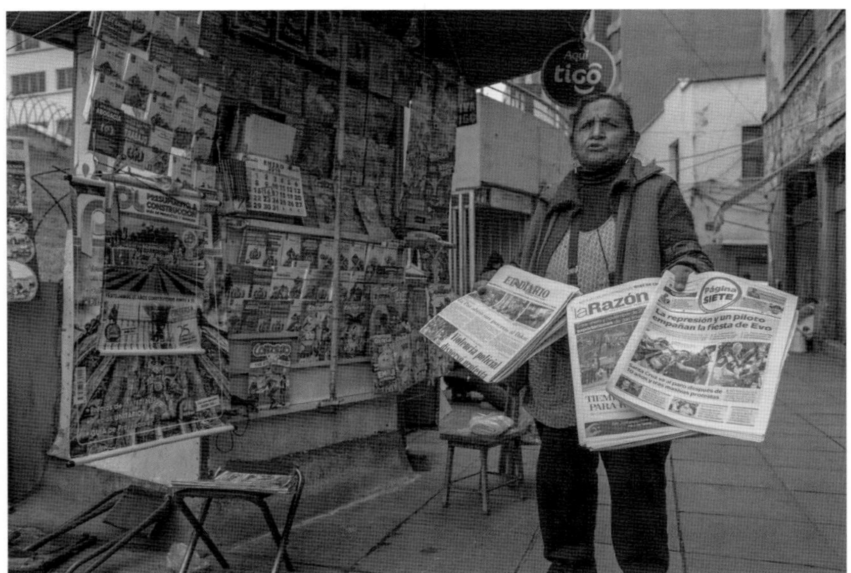

GONZALO PARDO FOR THE NEW YORK TIMES

Selling newspapers in La Paz, Bolivia's capital. The News Feed changes that Facebook has been testing in Bolivia and other countries play down nongovernmental news sources, limiting exposure to independent news reporting.

country's fourth-largest city, said Fabiola Chambi, the publication's web editor.

Ms. Chambi, however, fears the main consequence of the Explore function will be deepening polarization in a country already divided by ideology. "It's good to see things from your friends and your family, but there needs to be diversity of information," she said. "The miscellany is good."

Bolivia has also seen an increase in fake news as the established news sites are tucked behind the Explore function.

During nationwide judicial elections in December, one post widely shared on Facebook claimed to be from an election official saying votes would be valid only if an X was marked next to the candidate's name. Another post that day said government officials had put pens with erasable ink in the voting booths.

Vladimir Tirado, a social media expert in Bolivia, said the government might simply begin paying for posts to appear on users' News

KUNI TAKAHASHI FOR THE NEW YORK TIMES

The newsroom of The Daily News in Colombo, Sri Lanka. Sri Lanka is one of the countries where Facebook is testing News Feed changes amid a larger debate over its role in spreading fake news and misinformation.

Feeds, an option that he said most newsrooms could not afford.

"Whoever has more money will appear more," Mr. Tirado said. "In this sense, the government will certainly win."

Ms. Chambi of Los Tiempos said her newsroom hardly had enough money to pay its journalists to report stories, let alone to distribute them as paid posts on Facebook. The situation has left her uneasy about the role that the tech giant may play in her country.

"It's a private company — they have the right to do as they please, of course," she said. "But the first question we asked is 'Why Bolivia?' And we don't even have the possibility of asking why. Why us?"

CHAPTER 3

The Effects of Fake News

Fake news has real-world effects. Reactions to fake news can take the form of collective rage, or, if enough people see a false story, an unhinged individual who decides the response should be violent. Fake news strains the connections between people in a society, fragmenting otherwise functional disagreements and making reasonable dialogue impossible. In true fake-news fashion, however, sometimes the hype surrounding fake news as a phenomenon — fake news is destroying the world! — is overblown and probably sensationalized, as some social scientists have argued.

Media's Next Challenge: Overcoming the Threat of Fake News

BY JIM RUTENBERG | NOV. 6, 2016

THE LAST YEAR HAS turned the United States into a country of information addicts who compulsively check the television, the smartphone and the good old-fashioned newspaper with a burning question: What fresh twist could our national election drama and its executive producer, Donald J. Trump, possibly have in store for us now?

No doubt about it: Campaign 2016 has been a smash hit.

And to the news media have gone the spoils. With Mr. Trump providing must-see TV theatrics, cable news has drawn record audiences. Newspapers have reached online readership highs that would have been unimaginable just a few years ago.

On Wednesday comes the reckoning.

The election news bubble that's about to pop has blocked from plain view the expanding financial sinkhole at the center of the paper-and-ink branch of the news industry, which has recently seen a print advertising plunge that was "much more precipitous, to be honest with you, than anybody expected a year or so ago," as The Wall Street Journal editor in chief Gerard Baker told me on Friday.

Papers including The Journal, The New York Times, The Guardian, the Gannett publications and others have responded with plans to reorganize, shed staff, kill off whole sections, or all of the above.

Taken together, it means another rapid depletion in the nation's ranks of traditionally trained journalists whose main mission is to root out corruption, hold the powerful accountable and sort fact from fiction for voters.

It couldn't be happening at a worse moment in American public life. The internet-borne forces that are eating away at print advertising are enabling a host of faux-journalistic players to pollute the democracy with dangerously fake news items.

In the last couple of weeks, Facebook, Twitter and other social media outlets have exposed millions of Americans to false stories asserting that: the Clinton campaign's pollster, Joel Benenson, wrote a secret memo detailing plans to "salvage" Hillary Clinton's candidacy by launching a radiological attack to halt voting (merrily shared on Twitter by Roger Stone, an informal adviser to the Trump campaign); the Clinton campaign senior strategist John Podesta practiced an occult ritual involving various bodily fluids; Mrs. Clinton is paying public pollsters to skew results (shared on Twitter by Donald Trump Jr.); there is a trail of supposedly suspicious deaths of myriad Clinton foes (which The Times's Frank Bruni heard repeated in a hotel lobby in Ohio).

As Mike Cernovich, a Twitter star, alt-right news provocateur and promoter of Clinton health conspiracies, boasted in last week's New Yorker, "Someone like me is perceived as the new Fourth Estate." His content can live alongside that of The Times or The Boston Globe or The Washington Post on the Facebook newsfeed and be just as well read, if not more so. On Saturday he called on a President Trump to disband the White House press corps.

He may not have to. All you have to do is look at the effect of the Gannett cuts on its Washington staff, which Politico recently likened to a "blood bath."

Even before this year's ad revenue drop, the number of full-time daily journalists — nearly 33,000 according to the 2015 census conducted by the American Society of News Editors and the School of Journalism and Mass Communication at Florida International University — was on the way to being half what it was in 2000.

That contraction in the reporting corps, combined with the success of disinformation this year, is making for some sleepless nights for those in Washington who will have to govern in this bifurcated, real-news-fake-news environment.

"It's the biggest crisis facing our democracy, the failing business model of real journalism," Senator Claire McCaskill, Democrat of Missouri and a longtime critic of fake news, told me on Saturday.

Ms. McCaskill said that "journalism is partly to blame" for being slow to adjust as the internet turned its business model upside down and social media opened the competitive floodgates. "Fake news got way out ahead of them," she said.

It does not augur well for the future. Martin Baron, the Washington Post executive editor, said when we spoke last week, "If you have a society where people can't agree on basic facts, how do you have a functioning democracy?"

The cure for fake journalism is an overwhelming dose of good journalism. And how well the news media gets through its postelection hangover will have a lot to do with how the next chapter in the American political story is told.

That's why the dire financial reports from American newsrooms are so troubling. If the national reporting corps is going to be reduced even more during such an election-driven readership boom, what are things going to look like when the circus leaves town?

I surveyed the higher precincts of the industry last week, and what I found wasn't entirely gloomy; there was even some cause for optimism. But there's going to be a lot of nail-biting and some bloodletting on the way to deliverance.

It's pretty much taken as a given that the news audience will largely shrink next year, despite what is expected to be a compelling news environment.

"Is anything in 2017, politically speaking, going to be as sexy as it was in 2016? I'm not going to play poker at that table," Andrew Lack, the chairman of NBC News and MSNBC, told me on Friday.

Still, though he's predicting a ratings fall of 30 percent or perhaps "much more" at MSNBC, he said, "I don't have financial pressure on my bottom line."

That's not only because MSNBC and its competitors earned tens of millions of unexpected election-related dollars this year, but also because they still draw substantial income from cable subscriber fees.

Newspapers are the originators of that subscriber-advertising setup. But as lucrative print ads dwindle, and Facebook and Google gobble up more than two-thirds of the online advertising market, affecting digital-only outlets, too, newspapers are scrambling to build up their subscriber bases and break their reliance on print ads.

Mr. Baker of The Journal said he was confident that newspapers could make the transition but acknowledged a rough interim period that will require cuts and will be even harder to navigate or survive for smaller, regional papers (a practical invitation to municipal corruption).

The cause for relative optimism comes from the performance of some of the more ambitious, well-reported newspaper articles of the last year.

The Times article revealing Mr. Trump's nearly $1 billion tax loss in 1995 drew some 5.5 million page views. That's huge. The Washington Post doesn't share its numbers, but behold the more than 13,000 online comments attached to just one of David A. Fahrenthold's articles about how Mr. Trump ran his charity in ways that clashed with philanthropic moral conventions.

But in this new era, subscriber numbers are more important than fly-by-night readership.

Arthur Gregg Sulzberger, The Times's newly named deputy publisher, pointed to a bright spot in last week's earnings report. Mixed in with a 19-percent drop in print advertising revenue (!) was a 21 percent increase in digital advertising and, more important, the addition of 116,000 new digital-only subscriptions. The Times now has nearly 1.6 million subscribers to its digital-only offerings.

"It shows people are willing to pay for great, original, deeply reported and expert journalism," Mr. Sulzberger said. "That will allow great journalism to thrive."

It could be Pollyannaish to think so, but maybe this year's explosion in fake news will serve to raise the value of real news. If so, it will be great journalism that saves journalism.

"People will ultimately gravitate toward sources of information that are truly reliable, and have an allegiance to telling the truth," Mr. Baron said. "People will pay for that because they'll realize they'll need to have that in our society."

As The Times's national political correspondent Jonathan Martin wrote on Twitter last week, "Folks, subscribe to a paper. Democracy demands it."

Or don't. You'll get what you pay for.

How Fake News Turned a Small Town Upside Down

BY CAITLIN DICKERSON | SEPT. 26, 2017

ON A TUESDAY MORNING in June 2016, Nathan Brown, a reporter for The Times-News, the local paper in Twin Falls, Idaho, strolled into the office and cleared off a spot for his coffee cup amid the documents and notebooks piled on his desk. Brown, 32, started his career at a paper in upstate New York, where he grew up, and looks the part of a local reporter, clad in a fresh oxford and khakis that tend to become disheveled over the course of his long days. His first order of business was an article about a City Council meeting from the night before, which he hadn't attended. Brown pulled up a recording of the proceedings and began punching out notes for his weekly article. Because most governing in Twin Falls is done by a city manager, these meetings tend to deal with trivial subjects like lawn-watering and potholes, but Brown could tell immediately that this one was different.

"We have been made aware of a situation," said the first speaker, an older man with a scraggly white beard who had hobbled up to the lectern. "An alleged assault of a minor child and we can't get any information on it. Apparently, it's been indicated that the perpetrators were foreign Muslim youth that conducted this — I guess it was a rape." Brown recognized the man as Terry Edwards. About a year earlier, after The Times-News reported that Syrian refugees would very likely be resettled in Twin Falls, Edwards joined a movement to shut the resettlement program down. The group circulated a petition to put the proposal before voters. They failed to get enough signatures to force a referendum, but Brown was struck by how much support around town the movement attracted. In bars after work, he began to overhear conversations about the dangers of Islam. One night, he heard a man joke about dousing the entrance to the local mosque with pig's blood.

After he finished watching the video, Brown called the police chief, Craig Kingsbury, to get more information about the case. Kingsbury said that he couldn't discuss it and that the police reports were sealed because minors were involved. Brown made a couple phone calls: to the mayor and to his colleague at the paper who covers crime. He pieced together that 12 days earlier, three children had been discovered partly clothed inside a shared laundry room at the apartment complex where they lived. There were two boys, a 7-year-old and a 10-year-old, and a 5-year-old girl. The 7-year-old boy was accused of attempting some kind of sex act with the 5-year-old, and the 10-year-old had used a cellphone borrowed from his older brother to record it. The girl was American and, like most people in Twin Falls, white. The boys were refugees; Brown wasn't sure from where. In his article about the meeting, Brown seems to anticipate that the police chief's inability to elaborate was not going to sit well with the people whose testimony he had just watched.

That weekend, Brown was on his way to see a movie when he received a Facebook message from Jim Dalos Jr., a 52-year-old known to Twin Falls journalists and police as Scanner Man. Dalos is disabled; he works six hours a week as a dishwasher at a pizzeria but spends most of his time in his apartment, sitting in a reclining chair and drinking Diet Pepsi out of a 52-ounce plastic mug, voraciously consuming news. He reads the local paper, old issues of which litter his living-room floor, and keeps the television blaring — usually Fox News. He got his nickname because he constantly monitors an old police scanner, a gift he received as a teenager from his father, and often calls in tips to the media based on what he hears. He also happens to live at the apartment complex, Fawnbrook, where the laundry-room incident occurred.

Dalos told Brown that he had seen the police around Fawnbrook and that the victim's mother told him that the boys had been arrested. He also pointed Brown to a couple of Facebook groups that were created in response to the crime. Brown scrolled through them on his cellphone and saw links flying back and forth with articles that said that the little girl had been gang raped at knife point, that the perpetrators were Syrian refugees and that their fathers had celebrated with them afterward by giving them high fives. The stories also claimed that the City Council and the police department were conspiring to bury the crime.

Over the weekend, Brown plowed through his daily packs of cigarettes as he watched hundreds, then thousands, of people joining the groups. Their panic appeared to be piqued by a mass shooting, the deadliest in American history, that had just occurred at Pulse nightclub in Orlando. The perpetrator had declared allegiance to ISIS. The commenters also posted stories that claimed refugees were responsible for a rash of rapes in Europe and that a similar phenomenon in the United States was imminent. "My girl is blond and blue-eyed," one woman wrote. "I am extremely worried about her safety."

The details of the Fawnbrook case, as it became known, were still unclear to Brown, but he was skeptical of what he was reading. For one thing, he knew from his own previous reporting that no Syrians had been resettled in Twin Falls after all. He woke up early on Monday to get a head start on clarifying things as much as possible in order to write a follow-up article. Before he got into the office, a friend texted him, telling him to check the Drudge Report. At the top, a headline screamed: "REPORT: Syrian 'Refugees' Rape Little Girl at Knifepoint in Idaho."

As the only city of any size for 100 miles in any direction, Twin Falls serves as a modest hub within southern Idaho's vast agricultural sprawl. Its population of about 45,000 nearly doubles each day as people travel there to work, primarily in the thriving agribusinesses. But its bucolic rhythms still allow for children to play outside unattended and make driving a meditative experience. Surrounding the city and sprinkled among its tidy tract neighborhoods, potatoes, alfalfa, sugar beets and corn grow in fields. Half a million dairy cows in the area produce three-quarters of the state's milk supply. Because of its location, Twin Falls is home to major food processors like Chobani Yogurt, Clif Bar and Glanbia Nutritionals, a dairy company. All have large facilities in town and have helped to push down the unemployment rate to just under 3 percent, below the national average. The wealth of easy-to-find low-skilled jobs made Twin Falls attractive as a place for resettling refugees, and they began arriving in the 1980s, at that time mostly from Cambodia and the former Yugoslavia. Nearly 2,500 refugees have moved to the town over the years.

Most Twin Falls residents are churchgoing, and about half of those are Mormons. Locally owned stores and restaurants are generally closed on Sundays, and the city has not voted for a Democratic presidential candidate since Franklin Delano Roosevelt in 1936. Liberals often register as Republicans just to have an opportunity to participate in the electoral process, by voting in the primaries. If a Republican is going to win regardless, the thinking goes, they would at least like to play a role in deciding which one prevails.

The same qualities that bind the townspeople together can, in turn, be alienating to newcomers. The refugee community has begun to experience this effect as its demographic makeup has changed. Over the past decade and a half, as conflict spread across North Africa and the Middle East, Twin Falls started to resettle larger numbers of refugees with darker skin who follow an unfamiliar religion — two things that make it difficult to blend into a town that is 80 percent white.

On a national scale, an ascendant network of anti-Muslim activists and provocateurs has exploited the fears brought on by these changes, finding a platform and a receptive audience online. The narrative they espouse — on blogs with names like Jihad Watch — is that America, currently 1 percent Muslim, is in the midst of an Islamic invasion. Central to the worldview of these bloggers, some of whom have celebrity-size social-media followings, is that Muslims have a propensity toward sexual violence. They seize on any news item that bolsters this notion. Perhaps their biggest touchstone is an incident that took place in Cologne, Germany, on New Year's Eve in 2015. Mobs of men, many of them asylum seekers from the Middle East, pick-pocketed and groped more than a thousand women in and around a train station. The

German police acknowledged the incident had taken place only under pressure, as the women's stories began to leak out through the media. This established, for these activists, the contours of a narrative that they believe has been repeating itself. The Fawnbrook incident quickly drew their interest.

What happened in Twin Falls was sadly somewhat commonplace but not in the way the activists believed. The local Police Department investigates sex crimes on a weekly basis, and in about half a dozen of those that proceed to court each year, the victims and the accused are both minors. "If it's younger kids, it's them being curious," J.R. Paredez, the lead investigator on the case, explained to me. Some children who act out sexually have been victimized themselves, he said, while others have been exposed to explicit material at home or at school or, as is more common recently, on their cellphones. "As they start to get older, there's more of the actual sexual component to it."

Two weeks after the incident, the boys were charged with lewd and lascivious behavior against a minor. (The 14-year-old who lent his cellphone to the boys was initially charged with the same crime. He was not present in the laundry room, and his charge was eventually reduced to make him an accessory.) In Idaho, this statute applies to physical contact "done with the intent of arousing, appealing to, or gratifying the lust or passions or sexual desires of such person, such minor child, or third party." Paredez said that the cellphone video made clear what specifically had happened between the children, but that he couldn't show it to the reporters who asked him about it, because doing so would have constituted criminal distribution of child pornography. He called most of the details that he read about the case on the internet "100 percent false, like not even close to being accurate." (The family of the accused declined to comment.)

As more time passed without a solid account of what happened inside the laundry room, lurid rumors continued to surface online and came to dominate conversations in grocery stores and at school events. And while the City Council members did not have control over the case, the bloggers who wrote about it placed much of the blame on them.

On the Monday when Twin Falls was the top story on Drudge, the City Council held another weekly meeting. Normally only a handful of people attend, and Brown is one of the few reporters among them. But that night, the auditorium filled until there was standing room only, and television news crews appeared from Boise and other nearby cities. When it came time for public comments, one man got up and praised the city's handling of the case, followed by more than a dozen others who laid into the council members. Terry Edwards handed each of them a small copy of the Constitution and told them to do their jobs. A woman named Vicky Davis, her hair in a satiny white bob, stood up and proclaimed that Islam had declared jihad on America.

"They are not compatible with our culture," she said. "They hate us. They don't want to be Americans. They don't want to assimilate. What do you need to see? What more proof do you need?"

This was a highly unusual meeting, but Brown wasn't exactly surprised. Several months earlier, when the anti-refugee activists began to organize, he started reading up to try to better understand their views. He picked up a book by Ann Coulter and began to follow the anti-refugee blogs. At the meeting, he felt as if he were hearing all that he had read being repeated aloud by his neighbors.

Kingsbury, the police chief, read from a statement while fumbling with a thicket of microphones piled onto the lectern by visiting reporters. In between exasperated breaths, he explained why he could not disclose the details of the incident but said that he could address some of the misinformation that was spreading online. There was no evidence of a knife, he said, or of any celebration afterward or of a cover-up, and no Syrians were involved: The boys were from Sudan and Iraq. "I'm a kid who grew up in Idaho," he said. "Law enforcement takes these types of allegations very seriously. However, we can't act on them within an hour. It's not like a crime show." He told the audience that the boys had been arrested, to applause.

But online, Kingsbury's words only inflamed the activists more. Just after midnight, someone posted his work email address on Jihad Watch, along with those of the council members and the mayor. A commenter on another website called The Muslim Issue posted the phone numbers and email addresses for the town's government officials, the head of the refugee-resettlement center and some administrators at the college, which runs the refugee resettlement program. From there, the information spread to more blogs and to the comments sections of far-right news outlets with massive audiences.

By 9 the next morning, messages were pouring into the inbox of the mayor of Twin Falls, Shawn Barigar, nearly every minute. Barigar grew up in a neighboring town and went to work in Boise as a television news anchor before moving back to start a family. His even keel and the air of sophistication he picked up while living in a comparatively big city have made him popular politically. He is left of the town on many social issues, which has made some of his constituents suspicious of him. But most of the people who contacted him that summer were from other states and even other countries. Some people demanded that the city pay for a new car and apartment for the victim and her family. Others said that local officials' attempts to correct inaccurate details about the incident were veiled efforts to suggest that no crime had occurred at all, in order to protect the refugees. Others accused him of being a "globalist," a word that has taken on many definitions but in this case meant he was part of a vast, arcane conspiracy. They believed that establishment politicians wanted to turn red states like Idaho blue by starting wars and then importing refugees from those war zones as cheap labor who would not only displace American workers but also reliably vote Democratic.

Many of the people who wrote to the mayor had a much simpler goal: to unleash their hatred of Islam. One message, with the subject line "Muslims," said that refugees were committing rapes and hit-and-runs and urinating on women and that the mayor was guilty of treason. "It's out of the bag, [expletive]," it read. "We will and are holding you responsible for any and all crimes committed by these quote refugees. No courts. No police. Just us. You will answer to us in the darkness of night."

The next day, Camille Barigar, the mayor's wife, arrived in her office at the college, where she ran the performing-arts center, and started listening to her voice mail. In a calm, measured voice, a man who sounded as if he was reading from a script went on for nearly four minutes. "I wonder, Miss Barigar, if your residence was posted online and your whereabouts identified, how you would feel if half a dozen Muslim men raped and sodomized you, Miss Barigar, and when you tried to scream, broke every tooth in your mouth," he said. "And then I wonder how you'd feel if, when you went to the Twin Falls Police Department, they told you to run along, that this is simply cultural diversity."

The caller said that life was "becoming difficult" in the United States, just as it had in England. He referenced Jo Cox, a British member of Parliament who spoke out in support of refugees and later "met with opposition in the form of a bullet to the head."

"She's dead now," he said. "They've buried her."

The Twin Falls story aligned perfectly with the ideology that Stephen Bannon, then the head of Breitbart News, had been developing for years, about the havoc brought on by unchecked immigration and Islamism, all of it backed by big-business interests and establishment politicians. Bannon latched onto the Fawnbrook case and used his influence to expand its reach. During the weeks leading up to his appointment in August 2016 to lead Donald J. Trump's campaign for president, Twin Falls was a daily topic of discussion on Bannon's national radio show, where he called it "the beating heart" of all that the coming presidential election was about. He sent his lead investigative reporter, Lee Stranahan, to the town to investigate the case, boasting to his audience that Stranahan was a "pit bull" of a reporter. "We're going to let him off the chain," he said.

Then 50, Stranahan was relatively new to journalism. He had spent a few decades as a television producer and a graphic illustrator in Los

Angeles, and on the side he shot erotic photography, which is how he met his wife. Stranahan's transition into journalism began during the television writers' strike of 2007 and 2008. To keep himself entertained, he created parody political advertisements and posted them on YouTube. One of the first was a satirical Rudy Giuliani ad, asking Republican primary voters to support him because he had taken good care of his mistress, offering her private security courtesy of the N.Y.P.D., whereas Mitt Romney "didn't even bother" to take on a paramour. Stranahan says that within weeks, the videos led to invitations to appear on CNN and to meet with a vice president at NBC and to a job offer, which he accepted, writing political comedy for The Huffington Post.

In college, Stranahan was a libertarian and even attended Ayn Rand's funeral. But when he moved to California, he became a liberal, vehemently opposing the Iraq war and the presidency of George W. Bush. He voted for Barack Obama in 2008. Two years later, Stranahan interviewed Andrew Breitbart, a fellow Huffington Post alumnus, for an article he was writing about Jon Stewart's Rally to Restore Sanity and/or Fear. They spoke for more than three hours, bonding over their shared love of Depeche Mode. Eventually, Breitbart became Stranahan's mentor, converted him to conservatism and offered him a job. In 2011, Breitbart took Stranahan to the Conservative Political Action Conference and introduced him to Michele Bachmann, who, in Stranahan's recollection, convinced him that she had uncovered disturbing details about Islam that no one in the establishment was willing to talk about. Stranahan says this conversation was the genesis of his concerns about the religion.

Stranahan arrived in Idaho in August, after covering the national party conventions. The sealed nature of the case prevented any journalist from an exhaustive examination, and the accused and the victim's families refused to speak to the mainstream media. But Stranahan thrived in the void of facts. He was granted one of the few interviews with the victim's family, but his account of the crime offered little more information than others' had — and far more inaccuracies, according to the police and the county prosecutor. He described what took place as a "horrific gang rape" and wrote graphic details about the incident, which the Twin Falls Police say are untrue. On Breitbart radio, Stranahan openly wondered whether Barigar, the mayor, was "a big, you know, Shariah supporter." And he suggested repeatedly that mass rapes by refugees had occurred in Europe and were inevitably coming to the United States. "If you want to wait until your country turns into France or Cologne, Germany. If you want to wait, you can wait," he warned the audience. "But if you want to watch it and stop it now, you've got a chance to do it in November."

Stranahan says his Breitbart editors sent him to Twin Falls to report on the "Muslim takeover" of the town. (Breitbart denies this and says it's "absurd.") But he soon became enamored of a grander theory about what was happening in southern Idaho: globalism. He wrote that local businesses received government kickbacks for employing foreigners instead of Americans. (Stranahan did not cite any evidence of this, and it is untrue, according to the state Department of Labor.) And he often referred to a Syrian refugee crisis, though no Syrians were ever resettled there. Then, to bring the story full circle, he claimed these Muslim refugees were being used to replace American workers and that the government, big business and law enforcement were either conspiring to conceal the sexual-assault case or intentionally looking the other way, in order to keep the machine turning.

"Bottom line, this is bad for business," he told me in an interview last winter, explaining his interpretation of the city officials' rationale: " 'I'm not really going to look into this too deeply because if I find out the truth, if I discover what actually happened, if I figure out the truth, it's not really good for business.' " Stranahan believed that Chobani, a Greek-yogurt company, was at the center of the scheme. Breitbart had been covering the company for months, ever since the owner, Hamdi Ulukaya, a Turkish-born businessman, made a speech at the World Economic Forum at Davos encouraging other chief executives to pledge financial and political support to refugees.

While he was in town, Stranahan embedded with critics of the refugee program. They drove him to some of his interviews and to the yogurt factory to shoot drone footage. Stranahan doesn't get around well on his own in part because he has been mostly blind in one eye since grade school, when a neighborhood kid threw a rock at him, shattering his right optic nerve. Rather than a round pupil, his is jagged-edged, and so large that it nearly covers his iris. He shuffles when he walks because of neuropathic foot pain from diabetes, which he regulates by eating a ketogenic diet, usually one meal a day, consisting entirely of protein and fat. In Twin Falls, he subsisted most days on blackened chicken from Popeyes.

During the three months he was in Twin Falls, City Council members refused his interview requests, leaving him stuck inside an echo chamber with the activists, which he amplified online. When I was in Twin Falls, I found myself empathizing: These same activists refused to speak with me. One of the most outspoken among them is a woman named Julie DeWolfe, who lives atop a grassy hill 20 minutes outside town and who spent significant time with Stranahan. When I went there to ask for an interview, she came outside with several barking dogs and told me to leave. "The company you work for is not trustworthy," she said.

As the summer came to a close, The Times-News was bombarded with threatening phone calls and email from all over. After it received a threat that was deemed credible enough to engage the F.B.I., the editor of the paper told Brown and the other reporters to conduct their interviews outside the office and ordered the entire staff to walk in pairs when going out to their cars. For months, the reporters covered protests around town, which were widely hyped on social media but, for the most part, sparsely attended. At least once the Police Department deployed plainclothes officers into the crowds, with instructions to look after the journalists. Later, it turned out that fake Facebook accounts linked to the Russian government helped to spread stories about Twin Falls and even organized one of the rallies there. The event

Stranahan cut me off. "Hey, I'm walking into the White House right now," he said. He had just arrived for a press briefing with the president's spokesman. "Let me call you back."

This April, the boys accused in the Fawnbrook case admitted guilt — the juvenile court equivalent to pleading guilty — and were sentenced in June. The judge prohibited city officials from commenting on the outcome of the trial, but juvenile-justice experts told me that the boys would most likely be placed on probation and required to attend mandatory therapy to correct their behavior. Even in Idaho, a state with tough sentencing requirements, the law bars anyone under 10 from being jailed and only allows it in extreme cases for anyone under 12.

Late one Monday night in June I received a phone call from Dalos, the Scanner Man. He asked if I had heard about the "fireworks flying around Twin Falls." The news of the boys' fate had somehow reached the public. "The suspects didn't go to jail or nothing," he said, adding that people in town were "irate." Facebook posts about the story were again flooding his feed. "They're blaming it on Muslim law," he said. One of the articles circulating, from a site called Bare Naked Islam, included a photograph of the judge in the case with a large red arrow pointing toward his head, next to the caption "Corrupt Judge." Another article published the judge's home address and phone number, inciting another flood of harassment, a year after the initial onslaught.

Shawn and Camille Barigar's bickering has subsided, but they have discovered that they disagree over whether Islamic teachings conflict with American social norms. "I can't take the leap," Shawn told me, "that because you are Muslim therefore you are reading the Quran verbatim, and you're going to go out and do genital mutilation." Camille said she supported the local resettlement program but thought that her husband's unwillingness to even consider cultural differences or acknowledge any nuance was naïve. "I think we've got to be careful," she said. "And I don't want to be afraid to talk about it entirely or, like, sound racist." It is precisely this discomfort that provides an opening for people like Stranahan to dominate the conversation.

Part of the reason a fear of Islam has persisted in Twin Falls is because the local leadership refused to defuse it, according to Matt Christensen, 36, the editor of The Times-News. While Brown wrote articles that sorted out the truth about the Fawnbrook case, Christensen was publishing commentary that castigated the people who were spreading falsehoods. He told me that he had closed-door meetings with city officials, in which he asked them to write guest editorials doing the same, but none of them did. Christensen suspected that they were afraid of one of the most reliable political dangers in the region, the same force that leads would-be Democrats there to register as Republicans: being outflanked on the right is the quickest way to lose your job.

"Behind closed doors, they would all tell you they were pro-refugee, and we wanted them to step forward and make that declaration in a public arena, and it just never really happened," he told me. "That was frustrating to us especially at the beginning because it really felt like the newspaper was out there all alone." He continued: "There were days where we felt like, Godammit, what are we doing here? We write a story and it's going to reach 50,000 people. Breitbart writes a story and it's going to reach 2, 3, 4, 5, 10 million people. What kind of a voice do we have in this debate?"

The refugee resettlement center received a dramatic increase in donations from local residents during the last year. But those in the town who support the program have often been drowned out by the relatively smaller, but louder, group of activists who oppose it. Brown said he expected to see an anti-Shariah bill introduced in the State Legislature when the next session starts in 2018. Bills like this, which try to bar Islamic law from being used in American courts, have been introduced in the past two years in Boise but never passed. He speculated that the momentum of the past year could force a different outcome. "There are a lot of people who feel like society is changing too quickly, like the community is changing too quickly," he told me. "And who view other people not like them or who don't speak their language as a threat or a sign that their culture is going to be weakened. And they want to do what they can to stop that."

reassure patrons that the threats against him and his business were just an online phenomenon. Now, thanks in part to Mr. Trump's advisers, fake news just got real.

Mr. Trump says he disavows hate campaigns by his supporters. Now that we're seeing the real-world impact of phony theories spread by General Flynn, does "disavow" mean reconsidering his choice of the general as national security adviser?

'Kompromat' and the Danger of Doubt and Confusion in a Democracy

BY AMANDA TAUB | JAN. 15, 2017

WASHINGTON — Since the emergence of an unverified dossier with salacious claims about President-elect Donald J. Trump, Americans have debated the ramifications of the arrival of "kompromat" as a feature of American politics.

But those debates — for example, over the ethics of publishing the dossier — have often framed this practice as little more than a political form of blackmail, and one particular to Russia.

In fact, kompromat is more than an individual piece of damaging information: It is a broader attempt to manufacture public cynicism and confusion in ways that target not just one individual but an entire society.

And although this practice tends to be associated with Russia — the word kompromat is a portmanteau of the Russian words for "compromising" and "information" — it is a common feature of authoritarian and semiauthoritarian nations around the world.

Specific leaks may take aim at powerful individuals, but in the longer term, kompromat serves the interests of the powerful, which is why it is often a tool of autocrats. By eroding the very idea of a shared reality, and by spreading apathy and confusion among a public that learns to distrust leaders and institutions alike, kompromat undermines a society's ability to hold the powerful to account and ensure the proper functioning of government.

THE FOG OF DISINFORMATION

When Katy E. Pearce, a professor of communications at the University of Washington in Seattle, began studying access to technology in Azerbaijan, she expected to focus her research on how it could be a positive tool for promoting political freedom. But she changed her tack after encountering widespread fear of the ways that the government could use technology as a tool of repression.

"When I was interviewing people, it kept on coming up and coming up," she said. Kompromat is "a very cheap and easy way for the regime to demonstrate its power, and to harass people in a very visible way," she added.

That was a danger and a deterrent for the young activists she spoke to. But individual targets of kompromat are not its only victims, Professor Pearce said. It also harms society by diminishing public trust.

Thomas Rid, a professor of security studies at King's College London, wrote on Twitter that disinformation campaigns have "often deliberately blended accurate and forged details" to sow distrust and confusion.

If the news media and public figures publicize lies, they lose their credibility as trustworthy sources of information. "There's no reliable truth to rest upon," Professor Pearce said. "Every piece of information you get is 'possibly true, possibly false.' "

Degrading that trust can be deeply damaging. While in Russia in 2015, I was struck by how many of the people I met saw the world through a lens that I began to call the "prudent hypothetical." They reacted to all information, whether from official sources or thirdhand rumors, as if it might be true. I came to realize that it was a self-protective impulse, a way to prepare for any potential outcome in an unpredictable, unreliable world.

But they were also careful not to rely on that information, lest it turn out to be a fabrication. They trusted only the facts they had verified themselves, and only the people to whom they had close personal ties.

I had seen the same thing in Guatemala several years earlier. There, spreading lies and salacious gossip to discredit one's enemies is referred to as a "campaña negra," or a black campaign, rather than kompromat. But the result was the same: Public trust had been so eroded that lies were equally capable of destroying the honest and rehabilitating the criminal.

When it appeared that Yasmín Barrios, the judge presiding over the trial of Gen. Efraín Ríos Montt, Guatemala's former dictator, might convict him of genocide and crimes against humanity in 2013, a campaign of coordinated leaks and rumors portrayed her as a corrupt agent of foreign governments, willing to discredit her country in exchange for personal gain. Leaks and rumors attacked Judge Barrios personally, but by extension, they also undermined the credibility of the justice system in which she worked.

For example, the news media reported that the judge had been seen dining with "foreign women" at a restaurant in Guatemala City, and suggested that this was evidence of foreign influence on her rulings. In fact, the "foreigners" were Judge Barrios's Guatemalan mother, her neighbor, and a nun who was a friend of the family. But the rumors had their desired effect: They discredited not only Judge Barrios but also the genocide trial.

The Guatemalans I met knew that the stories they heard through the news media might be part of disinformation campaigns. But lacking better options, many still saw the world through the lens of the prudent hypothetical, viewing everything as possible and nothing as certain.

When General Ríos Montt was eventually convicted, many saw him as a victim of foreign machinations rather than a perpetrator of genocide and crimes against humanity. (His conviction was later vacated on procedural grounds.)

FOSTERING UNCERTAINTY AND DIVISION

Professor Pearce said she saw parallels between the use of kompromat overseas and recent news in the United States.

Although the Trump dossier purported to be a warning about kompromat elsewhere, she said, it could also be seen as a form of kompromat itself. She listed the parallels to what she had seen in her research: Its content is damaging but unverified. Its distribution was multilayered, with a website — in this case, BuzzFeed — publishing the unverified material and other outlets amplifying its impact by reporting on the ensuing controversy.

The document also fostered uncertainty and division. Masha Gessen, a Russian journalist, wrote in a recent opinion column in The New York Times that the release of the dossier had allowed Mr. Trump to say that "there was no such thing as truth, only a battle of opinions proffered by different actors, each of whom strives to be loudest." For some Americans, the dossier sowed concern about Mr. Trump's vulnerability to Russian influence. Others saw its publication as evidence that Mr. Trump was the victim of a disinformation campaign.

That may ultimately be to Mr. Trump's benefit if better-supported allegations against him arise in the future.

Americans were similarly divided in their views on the hacking of the Democratic National Committee's computer system. When Russian hackers leaked emails stolen from the committee, some saw it as evidence that Hillary Clinton, the Democratic presidential nominee, was a victim of foreign machinations, while others viewed the documents' content as confirmation that Mrs. Clinton was unreliable and dishonest. The leaks distracted from more substantive campaign issues and fueled public distrust and rancor.

Many people in the United States traditionally see the leak of confidential documents by whistle-blowers, like Daniel Ellsberg's release of the Pentagon Papers, as a way to hold the powerful to account. We tend to believe that transparency serves the public good, and secrecy the interests of the powerful.

Such a belief presumes that there is a fixed quantity of hidden information out there that the news media is or is not revealing. But in a kompromat society, incriminating material, real and fake, will be manufactured as needed to serve a political purpose.

To smear a president, undermine a judge or sow distrust in an institution or process, all someone needs to do is create a set of documents salacious enough to attract discussion, persuade some corner of the web to publish them and then wait for the resulting controversy to be reported as news.

That does not hold the powerful to account. And worse, it undermines the institutions that are supposed to do so.

In the United States, Professor Pearce said, "grabbing on and holding to the truth is becoming more challenging." If kompromat becomes a more widespread tactic, public trust will erode even further.

"A lot of the things that are good about the U.S. are because we have this kind of truth-based scaffolding," she said. "I don't want to live in an environment where I'm having to really be skeptical of everything, like people in authoritarian regimes have to be."

"Living like that is horrible," she said. "It is exhausting."

The Real Story About Fake News Is Partisanship

BY AMANDA TAUB | JAN. 11, 2017

IN HIS FAREWELL ADDRESS as president Tuesday, Barack Obama warned of the dangers of uncontrolled partisanship. American democracy, he said, is weakened "when we allow our political dialogue to become so corrosive that people of good character are turned off from public service, so coarse with rancor that Americans with whom we disagree are not just misguided, but somehow malevolent."

That seems a well-founded worry. Partisan bias now operates more like racism than mere political disagreement, academic research on the subject shows. And this widespread prejudice could have serious consequences for American democracy.

The partisan divide is easy to detect if you know where to look. Consider the thinly disguised sneer in most articles and editorials about so-called fake news. The very phrase implies that the people who read and spread the kind of false political stories that swirled online during the election campaign must either be too dumb to realize they're being duped or too dishonest to care that they're spreading lies.

But the fake-news phenomenon is not the result of personal failings. And it is not limited to one end of the political spectrum. Rather, Americans' deep bias against the political party they oppose is so strong that it acts as a kind of partisan prism for facts, refracting a different reality to Republicans than to Democrats.

Partisan refraction has fueled the rise of fake news, according to researchers who study the phenomenon. But the repercussions go far beyond stories shared on Facebook and Reddit, affecting Americans' faith in government — and the government's ability to function.

THE POWER OF PARTISAN BIAS

In 2009, Sean Westwood, then a Stanford Ph.D. student, discovered that partisanship was one of the most powerful forces in American life. He got annoyed with persistent squabbles among his friends, and he noticed that they seemed to be breaking along partisan lines, even when they concerned issues that ostensibly had nothing to do with politics.

"I didn't expect political conflict to spill over from political aspects of our lives to nonpolitical aspects of our lives, and I saw that happening in my social group," said Mr. Westwood, now a professor at Dartmouth.

He wondered if this was a sign that the role of partisanship in American life was changing. Previously, partisan conflict mostly applied to political issues like taxes or abortion. Now it seemed, among his acquaintances at least, to be operating more like racism or sexism, fueling negative or positive judgments on people themselves, based on nothing more than their party identification.

Curious, Mr. Westwood looked at the National Election Study, a long-running survey that tracks Americans' political opinions and behavior. He found that until a few decades ago, people's feelings about their party and the opposing party were not too different. But starting in the 1980s, Americans began to report increasingly negative opinions of their opposing party.

Since then, that polarization has grown even stronger. The reasons for that are unclear. "I suspect that part of it has to do with the rise of constant 24-hour news," Mr. Westwood said, "and also the shift that we've unfortunately gone through in which elections are more or less now a permanent state of affairs."

To find out more about the consequences of that polarization, Mr. Westwood, along with Shanto Iyengar, a Stanford professor who studies political communication, embarked on a series of experiments. They found something quite shocking: Not only did party identity turn out to affect people's behavior and decision making broadly, even on apolitical subjects, but according to their data it also had more influence on the way Americans behaved than race did.

That is a sea change in the role of partisanship in public life, Mr. Westwood said.

"Partisanship, for a long period of time, wasn't viewed as part of who we are," he said. "It wasn't core to our identity. It was just an ancillary trait. But in the modern era we view party identity as something akin to gender, ethnicity or race — the core traits that we use to describe ourselves to others."

That has made the personal political. "Politics has become so important that people select relationships on that basis," Mr. Iyengar said. For instance, it has become quite rare for Democrats to marry Republicans, according to the same Westwood/Iyengar paper, which cited a finding in a 2009 survey of married couples that only 9 percent consisted of Democrat-Republican pairs. And it has become more rare for children to have a different party affiliation from their parents.

But it has also made the political personal. Today, political parties are no longer just the people who are supposed to govern the way you want. They are a team to support, and a tribe to feel a part of. And the public's view of politics is becoming more and more zero-sum: It's about helping their team win, and making sure the other team loses.

HOW PARTISAN BIAS FUELS FAKE NEWS

Partisan tribalism makes people more inclined to seek out and believe stories that justify their pre-existing partisan biases, whether or not they are true.

"If I'm a rabid Trump voter and I don't know much about public affairs, and I see something about some scandal about Hillary Clinton's aides being involved in an assassination attempt, or that story about the pope endorsing Trump, then I'd be inclined to believe it," Mr. Iyengar said. "This is reinforcing my beliefs about the value of a Trump candidacy."

And Clinton voters, he said, would be similarly drawn to stories that deride Mr. Trump as a demagogue or a sexual predator.

Sharing those stories on social media is a way to show public support for one's partisan team — roughly the equivalent of painting your face with team colors on game day.

"You want to show that you're a good member of your tribe," Mr. Westwood said. "You want to show others that Republicans are bad or Democrats are bad, and your tribe is good. Social media provides a unique opportunity to publicly declare to the world what your beliefs are and how willing you are to denigrate the opposition and reinforce your own political candidates."

Partisan bias fuels fake news because people of all partisan stripes are generally quite bad at figuring out what news stories to believe. Instead, they use trust as a shortcut. Rather than evaluate a story directly, people look to see if someone credible believes it, and rely on that person's judgment to fill in the gaps in their knowledge.

"There are many, many decades of research on communication on the importance of source credibility," said John Sides, a professor at George Washington University who studies political communication.

Partisan bias strongly influences whom people perceive as trustworthy. One of the experiments that Mr. Westwood and Mr. Iyengar conducted demonstrated that people are much more likely to trust members of their party. In that experiment, they gave study participants $10 and asked how much they wanted to give to another player. Whatever that second player received would be multiplied, and he or she would then have a chance to return some of the cash to the original player.

How much confidence would the participant have that the other player would give some of the money back? They found that participants gave more money if they were told the other player supported the same political party as they did.

Partisanship's influence on trust means that when there is a partisan divide among experts, Mr. Sides said, "you get people believing wildly different sets of facts."

BEYOND FAKE NEWS: HOW THE PARTISAN DIVIDE AFFECTS POLITICS

The fake news that flourished during the election is a noticeable manifestation of that dynamic, but it's not what experts like Mr. Iyengar and Mr. Westwood find most worrying. To them, the bigger concern is that the natural consequence of this growing national divide will be a feedback loop in which the public's bias encourages extremism among politicians, undermining public faith in government institutions and their ability to function.

Politicians "have an incentive to attack, to go after their opponents, to reveal to their own side that they are good members of the tribe, that they are saying all the right things," Mr. Iyengar said. "This is an incentive for Republicans and Democrats in Congress to behave in a hyperpartisan manner in order to excite their base."

That feeds partisan bias among the public by reinforcing the idea that the opposition is made up of bad or dangerous people, which then creates more demand for political extremism.

The result is an environment in which compromise and collaboration with the opposing party are seen as signs of weakness, and of being a bad member of the tribe.

"It's a vicious cycle," Mr. Iyengar said. "All of this is going to make policy-making and fact-finding more problematic."

He already sees it affecting politicians' partisan response to Russia's election interference, for instance: "The Republicans are going to resist the notion that there was an intervention by the Russians that may have benefited Trump, because it is an inconvenient act. Whereas the Democrats are obviously motivated to seize upon that as a plausible account of what occurred."

Mr. Westwood agreed. When Russia intervened in the American election, "for a lot of voters it was to help defeat Hillary Clinton, so it's not surprising that many Republicans see that as righteous."

"To be cliché, the enemy of my enemy is my friend," he said.

Already, partisan bias is undermining confidence in the last election. "We saw some symptoms of that in this last campaign," Mr. Iyengar said. "You begin to have doubts about the legitimacy of the election. And you begin to view the outcome as somehow contaminated or tainted. And you had all of Trump's comments about how he would not concede if the election went to Clinton, and then you had all the people demonstrating."

Now, "you have quite a few people who are willing to call into question an institution for centuries that has been sacrosanct," Mr. Iyengar said.

Mr. Westwood was even more pessimistic. "The consequences of that are insane," he said, "and potentially devastating to the norms of democratic governance."

"I don't think things are going to get better in the short term; I don't think they're going to get better in the long term. I think this is the new normal."

As Fake News Spreads Lies, More Readers Shrug at the Truth

BY SABRINA TAVERNISE | DEC. 6, 2016

HAM LAKE, MINN. — One morning last week, Larry Laughlin, a retired business owner, opened his shiny black Dell laptop and scrolled through Facebook.

Most of the posts were ordinary news stories from conservative sites: Donald J. Trump's deal with the Carrier company. The political tussle over the recount. But a few items were his guilty pleasures.

"I like this guy," said Mr. Laughlin, looking at a post by the conservative commentator and author Mark Dice.

Mr. Dice has promoted conspiracy theories that the Jade Helm military training exercise last year was preparation for martial law and that the Sept. 11 attacks were an "inside job." But Mr. Laughlin likes him for what he said was his humorous political commentary and his sarcastic man-on-the-street interviews.

"I just like the satisfaction," said Mr. Laughlin, who started his own business and lives in an affluent Twin Cities suburb. "It's like a hockey game. Everyone's got their goons. Their goons are pushing our guys around, and it's great to see our goons push back."

The proliferation of fake and hyperpartisan news that has flooded into Americans' laptops and living rooms has prompted a national soul-searching, with liberals across the country asking how a nation of millions could be marching to such a suspect drumbeat. But while some Americans may take the stories literally — like the North Carolina man who fired his gun in a Washington pizzeria on Sunday trying to investigate a false story spread online of a child-abuse ring led by Hillary Clinton — many do not.

The larger problem, experts say, is less extreme but more insidious. Fake news, and the proliferation of raw opinion that passes for news, is creating confusion, punching holes in what is true, causing a kind of fun-house effect that leaves the reader doubting everything, including real news.

That has pushed up the political temperature and increased polarization. No longer burdened with wrestling with the possibility that they might be wrong, people on the right and the left have become more entrenched in their positions, experts say. In interviews, people said they felt more empowered, more attached to their own side and less inclined to listen to the other. Polarization is fun, like cheering a goal for the home team.

"There are an alarming number of people who tend to be credulous and form beliefs based on the latest thing they've read, but that's not the wider problem," said Michael Lynch, a professor of philosophy at the University of Connecticut. "The wider problem is fake news has the effect of getting people not to believe real things."

TIM GRUBER FOR THE NEW YORK TIMES

Larry Laughlin, a retired business owner from Minnesota, said he felt alienated from conventional news media.

of people voted illegally. A similar story had circulated on the site of the conspiracy theorist Alex Jones some days before. For Clayton Montgomery, 57, a retired state department of transportation worker in Waynesville, N.C., the numbers may not be precisely right, but the broad outlines rang true.

"All of a sudden they got this big push of registered voters," Mr. Montgomery said, referring to California. "They were all illegals. The same thing in the state of Washington, Los Angeles and Houston, too."

He said that Mr. Jones, who has called the Sandy Hook massacre a hoax, "can get a little conspiratorial," but added that he "raises some very logical and important questions."

Mr. Montgomery has concerns about immigration. He lived for years in South Florida, where he had a painting business that was deeply affected by cheap labor from Hispanic immigrants.

"They can't say that these people are not taking jobs away from American citizens," he said. "They come up and they lowball. It hurts a lot of people."

Another story online alleged that Mexico had a wall along its southern border "with guard towers," Mr. Montgomery said, to keep "all these other countries from coming in." (Mr. Laughlin saw that one, too, but pointed out that the photograph that accompanied the story was from Israel.)

Mr. Montgomery pushed back: "Check it out, it's true!"

Mr. Montgomery said he was nostalgic for the news of old, when Walter Cronkite delivered it. But the reputation of the press has been tarnished, he said, and people are left to navigate the fractured landscape on their own.

The online content can be frustrating, with headlines that promise more than the story delivers.

He noted one with a headline along the lines of "The wait is over; Hillary's being indicted."

"But then you click and there's nothing in there about her being indicted," Mr. Montgomery said. "It's almost like looking at a menu in a restaurant. Oh, that sounds delicious, it sounds great, and then it's this teeny weeny thing you maybe get three bites of."

Fake and hyperpartisan news from the right has been more conspicuous than from the left, but both sides indulge. BuzzFeed analyses have found more on the right. Some purveyors have said right-leaning items are more profitable.

But the left has its share. The fact-checking site Snopes said it found no evidence for a quotation, often attributed to Mr. Trump by the left, that Republican voters were stupid.

That type of insult increases the partisan divide. Paul Indre, a project manager for a hardware goods company in Akron, Ohio, who gets his news from podcasts and television, avoids much of online news. But he understands why people go there in a polarized era.

Mr. Indre, a moderate Republican, said he remained vigilant against fake news.

"If I'm in a Trump group and someone will share something that's fake news," he said, "I'll ask them 'Hey did you check that?'"

But it is often impossible to tell whether "they are just lobbing a bomb, or do they really believe it?" he said. "You have some folks who are a little naïve, who don't follow the news and believe it. I mean, people do buy The National Enquirer and believe it."

"But some of it might be revenge factor, getting back at something they are hearing from the left," he said. "Maybe they are just reacting to something. Maybe we are just in this reactionary period."

'Fake News': Wide Reach but Little Impact, Study Suggests

BY BENEDICT CAREY | JAN. 2, 2018

FAKE NEWS EVOLVED from seedy internet sideshow to serious electoral threat so quickly that behavioral scientists had little time to answer basic questions about it, like who was reading what, how much real news they also consumed and whether targeted fact-checking efforts ever hit a target.

Sure, surveys abound, asking people what they remember reading. But these are only as precise as the respondents' shifty recollections and subject to a malleable definition of "fake." The term "fake news" itself has evolved into an all-purpose smear, used by politicians and the president to deride journalism they don't like.

But now the first hard data on fake-news consumption has arrived. Researchers last week posted an analysis of the browsing histories of thousands of adults during the run-up to the 2016 election — a real-time picture of who viewed which fake stories, and what real news those people were seeing at the same time.

The reach of fake news was wide indeed, the study found, yet also shallow. One in four Americans saw at least one false story, but even the most eager fake-news readers — deeply conservative supporters of President Trump — consumed far more of the real kind, from newspaper and network websites and other digital sources.

While the research can't settle the question of whether misinformation was pivotal in the 2016 election, the findings give the public and researchers the first solid guide to asking how its influence may have played out. That question will become increasingly important as online giants like Facebook and Google turn to shielding their users from influence by Russian operatives and other online malefactors.

"There's been a lot of speculation about the effect of fake news and a lot of numbers thrown around out of context, which get people exercised," said Duncan Watts, a research scientist at Microsoft who has argued that misinformation had a negligible effect on the election results. "What's nice about this paper is that it focuses on the actual consumers themselves."

In the new study, a trio of political scientists — Brendan Nyhan of Dartmouth College (a regular contributor to The Times's Upshot), Andrew Guess of Princeton University and Jason Reifler of the University of Exeter — analyzed web traffic data gathered from a representative sample of 2,525 Americans who consented to have their online activity monitored anonymously by the survey and analytic firm YouGov.

The data included website visits made in the weeks before and after the 2016 election, and a measure of political partisanship based on overall browsing habits. (The vast majority of participants favored Mr. Trump or Hillary Clinton.)

The team defined a visited website as fake news if it posted at least two demonstrably false stories, as defined by economists Hunt Allcott and Matthew Gentzkow in research published last year. On 289 such sites, about 80 percent of bogus articles supported Mr. Trump.

The online behavior of the participants was expected in some ways, but surprising in others. Consumption broke down along partisan lines: the most conservative 10 percent of the sample accounted for about 65 percent of visits to fake news sites.

Pro-Trump users were about three times more likely to visit fake news sites supporting their candidate than Clinton partisans were to visit bogus sites promoting her. Still, false stories were a small fraction of the participants' overall news diet, regardless of political preference: just 1 percent among Clinton supporters, and 6 percent among those pulling for Mr. Trump. Even conservative partisans viewed just five fake news articles, on average, over more than five weeks. There was no way to determine from the data how much, or whether, people believed what they saw on these sites. But many of these were patently absurd, like one accusing Mrs. Clinton of a "Sudden Move of $1.8 Billion to Qatar Central Bank," or a piece headlined "Video

Showing Bill Clinton With a 13-Year-Old Plunges Race Into Chaos."

"For all the hype about fake news, it's important to recognize that it reached only a subset of Americans, and most of the ones it was reaching already were intense partisans," Dr. Nyhan said.

"They were also voracious consumers of hard news," he added. "These are people intensely engaged in politics who follow it closely."

Given the ratio of truth to fiction, Dr. Watts said, fake news paled in influence beside mainstream news coverage, particularly stories about Mrs. Clinton and her use of a private email server as secretary of state. Coverage of that topic appeared repeatedly and prominently in venues like The New York Times and the Washington Post.

The new study does not rule out the possibility that fake news affected the elections, said David Rand, an associate professor of psychology, economics and management at Yale University.

Americans over age 60 were much more likely to visit a fake news site than younger people, the new study found. Perhaps confusingly, moderately left-leaning people viewed more pro-Trump fake news than they did pro-Clinton fake news.

One interpretation of that finding, Dr. Rand said, may be that older, less educated voters who switched from Obama in 2012 to Trump in 2016 were particularly susceptible to fake news.

"You can see where this might have had an impact in some of those close swing states, like Wisconsin," Dr. Rand said. "But this of course is a matter of conjecture, reasoning backward from the findings."

The study found that Facebook was by far the platform through which people most often navigated to a fake news site. Last year, in response to criticism, the company began flagging stories on its site that third-party fact-checkers found to make false claims with a red label saying "disputed."

Most people in the new study encountered at least some of these labels, but "we saw no instances of people reading a fake news article and a fact-check of that specific article," Dr. Nyhan said. "The fact-checking websites have a targeting problem."

In December, Facebook announced a change to its monitoring approach. Instead of labeling false stories, Facebook will surface the fact-checks along with the fake story in the user's news feed.

Fake News and Bots May Be Worrisome, but Their Political Power Is Overblown

OPINION | BY BRENDAN NYHAN | FEB. 13, 2018

HOW EASY IS IT to change people's votes in an election?

The answer, a growing number of studies conclude, is that most forms of political persuasion seem to have little effect at all.

This conclusion may sound jarring at a time when people are concerned about the effects of the false news articles that flooded Facebook and other online outlets during the 2016 election. Observers speculated that these so-called fake news articles swung the election to Donald J. Trump. Similar suggestions of large persuasion effects, supposedly pushing Mr. Trump to victory, have been made about online advertising from the firm Cambridge Analytica and content promoted by Russian bots.

Much more remains to be learned about the effects of these types of online activities, but people should not assume they had huge effects. Previous studies have found, for instance, that the effects of even television advertising (arguably a higher-impact medium) are very small. According to one credible estimate, the net effect of exposure to an additional ad shifts the partisan vote of approximately two people out of 10,000.

In fact, a recent meta-analysis of numerous different forms of campaign persuasion, including in-person canvassing and mail, finds that their average effect in general elections is zero.

Field experiments testing the effects of online ads on political candidates and issues have also found null effects. We shouldn't be surprised — it's hard to change people's minds! Their votes are shaped by fundamental factors like which party they typically support and how they view the state of the economy. "Fake news" and bots are likely to have vastly smaller effects, especially given how polarized our politics have become.

Here's what you should look for in evaluating claims about vast persuasion effects from dubious online content:

How many people actually saw the questionable material. Many alarming statistics have been produced since the election about how many times "fake news" was shared on Facebook or how many times Russian bots retweeted content on Twitter. These statistics obscure the fact that the content being shared may not reach many Americans (most people are not on Twitter and consume relatively little political news) or even many humans (many bot followers may themselves be bots).

Whether the people being exposed are persuadable. Dubious political content online is disproportionately likely to reach heavy news consumers who already have strong opinions. For instance, a study I conducted with Andrew Guess of Princeton and Jason Reifler of the University of Exeter in Britain showed that exposure to fake news websites before the 2016 election was heavily concentrated among the 10 percent of Americans with the most conservative information diets — not exactly swing voters.

The proportion of news people saw that is bogus. The total number of shares or likes that fake news and bots attract can sound enormous until you consider how much information circulates online. Twitter, for instance, reported that Russian bots tweeted 2.1 million times before the election — certainly a worrisome number. But these represented only 1 percent of all election-related tweets and 0.5 percent of views of election-related tweets.

Similarly, my study with Mr. Guess and Mr. Reifler found that the mean number of articles on fake news websites visited by Trump supporters was 13.1, but only 40 percent of his supporters visited such websites, and they represented only about 6 percent of the pages they visited on sites focusing on news topics.

None of these findings indicate that fake news and bots aren't worrisome signs for American democracy. They can mislead and polarize citizens, undermine trust in the media, and distort the content of public debate. But those who want to combat online misinformation should take steps based on evidence and data, not hype or speculation.

BRENDAN NYHAN IS A PROFESSOR OF GOVERNMENT AT DARTMOUTH COLLEGE.

CHAPTER 4

Donald Trump and Weaponizing Fake News

No one has successfully weaponized the term "fake news" as effectively as President Donald J. Trump. During his first year in office, "fake news" became President Trump's defense against allegations that he and his campaign staff worked with Russian agents to affect the outcome of the election. President Trump has used "fake news" to deflect accusations of sexual harassment, extra-marital affairs, obstruction of justice, suspicions of corruption, and the idea that his White House is chaotic. He popularized "fake news" as a political weapon, especially among right-wing conservatives and politicians.

10 Times Trump Spread Fake News

BY SAPNA MAHESHWARI | JANUARY 18, 2017

IN THE HEATED DISCUSSIONS over the effects of fake news on democracy and civil society, Donald J. Trump has often taken center stage.

He has used false claims to attack his political opponents, question the legitimacy and loyalty of the Obama administration and other Democrats, and undermine the news media, the federal government and other institutions that many of his supporters do not trust.

The practice has paralleled his rise from reality TV star to holder of the nation's highest elected office, according to an analysis of his social media activity.

When discussing some of his claims, Mr. Trump has cited as evidence articles posted through Breitbart News, manipulated YouTube videos and celebrity gossip publications like The National Enquirer.

Mr. Trump has also tweeted links from right-wing blogs like WND.com and TheRightScoop.com that often promote sensational conspiracy theories and contain little original reporting.

His sourcing highlights the bounty of misinformation accessible on the web and its power in a deeply divided America — especially when endorsed by someone of Mr. Trump's influence and visibility.

He offered this explanation for his actions while discussing an altered YouTube video he had tweeted as part of an unsubstantiated claim that a protester at one of his rallies had ties to the Islamic State: "I don't know what they made up; all I can do is play what's there," Mr. Trump said on NBC's "Meet the Press."

"All I know is what's on the internet."

Below are examples from the last several years of Mr. Trump's penchant for making fraudulent claims and backing them up with information gleaned from unsubstantiated sources.

THE AFFORDABLE CARE ACT AND 'DEATH PANELS'

ObamaCare does indeed ration care. Seniors are now restricted to "comfort care" instead of brain surgery. Repeal now! http://bit.ly/spcorH

— Donald J. Trump (@realDonaldTrump) Nov. 28, 2011

In November 2011, Mr. Trump proclaimed that the Affordable Care Act would "ration care," linking to an article on TheRightScoop.com. The story cited an anonymous caller's comments on a conservative radio talk show as proof the act established so-called death panels that would determine whether or not elderly patients received care.

The notion of death panels was deemed the "Lie of the Year" in 2009 by the fact-checking website PolitiFact, which traced its rise to

JOSH HANER/THE NEW YORK TIMES

Donald J. Trump demonstrating from his office in Trump Tower how he sends Twitter messages through his smartphone.

comments made by Sarah Palin on Facebook. The additional claims in the story Mr. Trump shared were debunked by the American Association of Neurological Surgeons and the Department of Health and Human Services, according to Snopes, another fact-checking website.

PRESIDENT OBAMA'S HOLIDAY MESSAGE

What a convenient mistake: @BarackObama issued a statement for Kwanza but failed to issue one for Christmas. http://bit.ly/vUmvpM

— Donald J. Trump (@realDonaldTrump) Dec. 28, 2011

Mr. Trump took to Twitter to share a story from TheGatewayPundit.com, a conservative blog, which falsely claimed that Mr. Obama had issued a statement for "the fake holiday" Kwanzaa but not for Christmas. (Mr. Obama's Christian faith has been questioned by political opponents; some have sought to assail the legitimacy of his presidency by falsely claiming he is a Muslim.) After the political blog Talking Points Memo refuted the story, Mr. Trump shared it again on Twitter, starting his post with "I'm right, TPM is wrong."

President Obama and his wife wished Americans a "merry Christmas" on Dec. 24, 2011, in a video address shared on Twitter, YouTube and the White House website. Earlier that month, Mr. Obama said he hoped Americans had "the merriest of Christmases," as his family lit the National Christmas Tree in front of the White House, and separately said that "the story of Jesus Christ changed the world" in remarks at the "Christmas in Washington" concert. The statement on Kwanzaa was in line with those made by George W. Bush through 2008.

BIRTHERISM

An 'extremely credible source' has called my office and told me that @BarackObama's birth certificate is a fraud.

— Donald J. Trump (@realDonaldTrump) Aug. 6, 2012

In March 2011, Mr. Trump started raising questions about President Obama's birthplace and birth certificate on television, on shows that included ABC's "The View" and NBC's "Today." The notion had been debunked and pushed to the realm of conspiracy theorists after Mr. Obama released his short-form birth certificate from the Hawaii Department of Health in 2008.

Mr. Trump also promoted his claims through Twitter, citing "an 'extremely credible source'" that called his office and allegedly told him the certificate was a fraud, as well as linking to posts on blogs like WND.com and FreedomOutpost.com. While Mr. Trump was roundly denounced for continuing to push the conspiracy theory, it solidified his connection to the largely white Republican base that was so instrumental in his election victory in November.

SECRET OIL DEAL TO CONTROL GAS PRICES

Mr. Trump has also made claims without supporting material of any kind. He once shared political views through a YouTube video series, "From The Desk Of Donald Trump," sounding off on the Republican Party and Mr. Obama, but also on topics as varied as Andy Roddick's talent and the state of the desk itself. ("Many people have been asking about my desk and the fact that I have so many papers on my desk," it began.) He tweeted links to the posts with the hashtag #trumpvlog throughout 2011 and 2012.

In April 2012, Mr. Trump posted a segment in which he said, "I have no doubt in my mind that President Obama made a deal with the Saudis to flood the markets with oil before the election so he can at least keep it down a little bit."

He added: "After the election it's going to be a mess. You're going to see numbers like you've never seen if he wins." He repeated this allegation about a secret deal on CNBC in June of that year, which Fox published under the headline "Trump: Obama's Secret Saudi Oil Deal to Win Re-election."

LINKING AUTISM TO VACCINATIONS

Autism rates through the roof–why doesn't the Obama administration do something about doctor-inflicted autism. We lose nothing to try.

— Donald J. Trump (@realDonaldTrump) Oct. 22, 2012

Starting in 2012, Mr. Trump has repeatedly expressed his personal belief that autism is linked to childhood vaccinations, saying it in interviews, on Twitter, and even during a Republican debate.

On the show "Fox & Friends" in April 2012, Mr. Trump was asked about the rising number of children with autism diagnoses and said, "I have a theory and it's a theory that some people believe in, and that's the vaccinations." Later in the segment, one host noted most doctors disagree and that studies do not show a link, which Mr. Trump acknowledged, adding, "It's also very controversial to even say, but I couldn't care less." He said he had seen changes in children firsthand to support his belief.

Plenty of studies, including a recent one that involved almost 100,000 children, have shown there is no scientific evidence linking vaccinations to autism, and that there is no benefit to delaying vaccinations. Instead, children who are not vaccinated on the regular schedule can be at risk for infectious diseases for a longer period. One doctor told Scientific American that "misinformation on the internet often frightens parents away from following" the vaccination schedule recommended by the Centers for Disease Control and Prevention, the only one endorsed by the American Academy of Pediatrics. In 2015, a measles outbreak in California, which started at Disneyland, was partly attributed to diseases spread by children who were not vaccinated.

In October 2012, Mr. Trump took to Twitter to ask why President Obama's administration was not intervening. He then wrote in March 2014, "If I were President I would push for proper vaccinations but would not allow one time massive shots that a small child cannot take - AUTISM."

QUESTIONING UNEMPLOYMENT DATA

The underemployment being quoted as 14.9% is way low–real number could be 20%.

— Donald J. Trump (@realDonaldTrump) July 13, 2012

Think of it—20% of our country is essentially unemployed.

— Donald J. Trump (@realDonaldTrump) July 13, 2012

Mr. Trump has a long history of casting doubt on the unemployment data and figures on "underemployment," a measure that also includes

The fact-checking website PolitiFact noted that "several historians of the period told us they've never seen Cruz's name come up in connection with Oswald."

PROTESTER WAS MEMBER OF ISIS

USSS did an excellent job stopping the maniac running to the stage. He has ties to ISIS. Should be in jail! https://amp.twimg.com/v/977860d3-6b1b-4a5f-a81e-67baa6e2e3b1 ...?ssr=true

— Donald J. Trump (@realDonaldTrump) March 12, 2016

Mr. Trump claimed at a rally last year that a man who charged him at another event was linked to the Islamic State, yet no government agency suggested the man was connected to ISIS or terrorism. He repeated the allegation in a tweet, linking to a video that claimed to show the man. It was overlaid with Arabic text and music and appeared to have been created as a hoax.

When asked on NBC's "Meet the Press" about the lack of evidence tying the man to ISIS and the video hoax, Mr. Trump did not seem deterred.

"He was dragging a flag along the ground and he was playing a certain type of music and supposedly there was chatter about ISIS," he responded. "What do I know about it?"

VOTER FRAUD

In addition to winning the Electoral College in a landslide, I won the popular vote if you deduct the millions of people who voted illegally

— Donald J. Trump (@realDonaldTrump) Nov. 27, 2016

After winning the presidential election but losing the popular vote, Mr. Trump took to Twitter to claim that he actually received more votes than Mrs. Clinton "if you deduct the millions of people who voted illegally." The notion was popularized by Infowars, a website replete with conspiracy theories that include questioning the shooting at Sandy Hook Elementary School.

The overwhelming consensus from people who oversaw the general election in states around the country was that the amount of voter fraud in 2016 was next to none.

White House Pushes 'Alternative Facts.' Here Are the Real Ones.

BY NICHOLAS FANDOS | JAN. 22, 2017

WASHINGTON — Kellyanne Conway, counselor to President Trump, said on NBC's "Meet the Press" on Sunday that the White House had put forth "alternative facts" to ones reported by the news media about the size of Mr. Trump's inauguration crowd.

She made this assertion — which quickly went viral on social media — a day after Mr. Trump and Sean Spicer, the White House press secretary, had accused the news media of reporting falsehoods about the inauguration and Mr. Trump's relationship with the intelligence agencies.

In leveling this attack, the president and Mr. Spicer made a series of false statements.

Here are the facts.

In a speech at the C.I.A. on Saturday, Mr. Trump said the news media had constructed a feud between him and the intelligence community. "They sort of made it sound like I had a 'feud' with the intelligence community," he said. "It is exactly the opposite, and they understand that, too."

In fact, Mr. Trump repeatedly criticized the intelligence agencies during his transition to office and has questioned their conclusion that Russia meddled in the election to aid his candidacy. He called their assessment "ridiculous" and suggested that it had been politically motivated.

After the disclosure of a dossier with unsubstantiated claims about him, Mr. Trump alleged that the intelligence agencies had allowed a leak of the material. "Are we living in Nazi Germany?" he asked in a post on Twitter.

Intelligence agencies should never have allowed this fake news to "leak" into the public. One last shot at me.Are we living in Nazi Germany?

— Donald J. Trump (@realDonaldTrump) Jan. 11, 2017

Mr. Trump said of his inauguration crowd, "It looked honestly like a million and a half people, whatever it was, it was, but it went all the way back to the Washington Monument."

Aerial photographs clearly show that the crowd did not stretch to the Washington Monument. An analysis by The New York Times, comparing photographs from Friday to ones taken of Barack Obama's 2009 inauguration, showed that Mr. Trump's crowd was significantly smaller and less than the 1.5 million people he claimed. An expert hired by The Times found that Mr. Trump's crowd on the National Mall was about a third of the size of Mr. Obama's in 2009.

Mr. Trump said that though he had been "hit by a couple of drops" of rain as he began his address on Inauguration Day, the sky soon cleared. "And the truth is, it stopped immediately, and then became sunny," he said. "And I walked off, and it poured after I left. It poured."

The truth is that it began to rain lightly almost exactly as Mr. Trump began to speak and continued to do so throughout his remarks, which lasted about 18 minutes, and after he finished.

Speaking later on Saturday in the White House briefing room, Mr. Spicer amplified Mr. Trump's false claims. "This was the largest audience to ever witness an inauguration — period — both in person and around the globe," he said.

There is no evidence to support this claim. Not only was Mr. Trump's inauguration crowd far smaller than Mr. Obama's in 2009, but he also drew fewer television viewers in the United States (30.6 million) than Mr. Obama did in 2009 (38 million) and Ronald Reagan did in 1981 (42 million), Nielsen reported. Figures for online viewership were not available.

Mr. Spicer said that Washington's Metro system had greater ridership on Friday than it did for Mr. Obama's 2013 inauguration. "We know that 420,000 people used the D.C. Metro public transit yesterday, which actually compares to 317,000 that used it for President Obama's last inaugural," Mr. Spicer said.

Neither number is correct, according to the transit system, which reported 570,557 entries into the rail system on Friday, compared with 782,000 on Inauguration Day in 2013.

Mr. Spicer said that "this was the first time in our nation's history that floor coverings have been used to protect the grass on the Mall. That had the effect of highlighting any areas where people were not standing, while in years past the grass eliminated this visual."

In fact, similar coverings were used during the 2013 inauguration to protect the grass. The coverings did not hamper analyses of the crowd size.

Mr. Spicer said that it was "the first time that fencing and magnetometers went as far back on the Mall, preventing hundreds of thousands of people from being able to access the Mall as quickly as they had in inaugurations past."

The Secret Service said security measures were largely unchanged this year. There were also few reports of long lines or delays.

‘Alternative Facts’ and the Costs of Trump-Branded Reality

BY JIM RUTENBERG | JAN. 22, 2017

WHEN DONALD J. TRUMP swore the presidential oath on Friday, he assumed responsibility not only for the levers of government but also for one of the United States’ most valuable assets, battered though it may be: its credibility.

The country’s sentimental reverence for truth and its jealously guarded press freedoms, while never perfect, have been as important to its global standing as the strength of its military and the reliability of its currency. It’s the bedrock of that “American exceptionalism” we’ve heard so much about for so long.

Disinformation was for dictatorships, banana republics and failed states.

Yet there it was on Saturday, emanating from the lectern of the White House briefing room — the official microphone of the United States — as Mr. Trump’s press secretary, Sean Spicer, used his first appearance there to put forth easily debunked statistics that questioned the news media’s reporting on the size of the president’s inaugural audience (of all things).

Mr. Spicer was picking up on the message from his boss, who made false claims about news coverage earlier that day as he declared a “running war” with the news media during a visit to the Central Intelligence Agency, whose most solemn duty is to feed vital and true information to presidents as they run actual wars.

It was chilling when Mr. Trump’s assertion that reporters were “among the most dishonest people on earth” became an applause line for the crowd gathered to hear him speak in front of the memorial to fallen agents at C.I.A. headquarters.

Still more chilling was when the White House senior adviser Kellyanne Conway appeared on “Meet the Press” on Sunday to assert that Mr. Spicer’s falsehoods were simply “alternative facts.”

DOUG MILLS/THE NEW YORK TIMES

Sean Spicer, the White House press secretary, during a briefing on Saturday. He used his first appearance to put forth easily debunked facts.

Ms. Conway made no bones about what she thought of the news media's ability to debunk those "alternative facts" in a way Americans — especially Trump-loving Americans — would believe.

"You want to talk provable facts?" she said to the moderator, Chuck Todd. "Look — you've got a 14 percent approval rating in the media, that you've earned. You want to push back on us?" (She appeared to be referring to a Gallup poll figure related to Republicans' views.)

And really, there it was: an apparent animating principle of Mr. Trump's news media strategy since he first began campaigning. That strategy has consistently presumed that low public opinion of mainstream journalism (which Mr. Trump has been only too happy to help stoke) creates an opening to sell the Trump version of reality, no matter its adherence to the facts.

As Mr. Trump and his supporters regularly note, whatever he did during the campaign, it was successful: He won. His most ardent supporters loved the news media bashing. And the complaints and aggressive fact-checking by the news media played right into his hands. He portrayed it as just so much whining and opposition from yet another overprivileged constituency of the Washington establishment.

But will tactics that worked in the campaign work in the White House? History is littered with examples of new administrations that quickly found that the techniques that served them well in campaigns did not work well in government.

And if they do work, what are the long-term costs to government credibility from tactical "wins" that are achieved through the aggressive use of falsehoods? Whatever they are, Mr. Trump should realize that it could hurt his agenda more than anything else.

There's a reason George W. Bush's adviser Karen Hughes told the newly promoted Bush press secretary, Scott McClellan, in 2003, "Your most important job, in my view, will be to make sure the president maintains his credibility with the American people."

"'It's one of his greatest strengths,'" Mr. McClellan quoted Ms. Hughes as saying in his autobiography, "What Happened."

Mr. McClellan's book chronicles how Mr. Bush staked that credibility on the false rationale for the Iraq invasion — that Saddam Hussein had weapons of mass destruction — and ultimately lost the confidence of Americans, hobbling him for the rest of his presidency.

But the damage wasn't isolated to Mr. Bush's political standing. To this day, the American intelligence community must contend with lingering questions about its own credibility — to wit, taunts from Moscow (not to mention from Mr. Trump) that assessments pointing to Russian meddling in the presidential election are questionable. After all, wasn't it wrong about Iraq?

There's a big difference in importance between the size of Mr. Trump's inaugural audience and the intelligence that led to war, no question. And, as the former Bush White House press secretary Ari Fleischer noted in a conversation with me on Sunday, it's way too early to say whether Mr. Spicer's weekend performance will be the norm.

The Trump team's emotions were raw over the weekend, Mr. Fleischer noted, after a mistaken pool report was sent to the rest of the White House press corps, claiming that Mr. Trump had removed a bust of the Rev. Dr. Martin Luther King Jr. from the Oval Office. Zeke Miller, the Time magazine journalist who had written the report, quickly corrected it and apologized when the White House alerted him to the error.

"It rightly leaves the people inside feeling that 'reporters were opposed to us all along for being racist and the first thing they did was imply we were,' " Mr. Fleischer said.

Still, the weekend's events did not arrive in a vacuum. There was the report last week in The Washington Post that the Smithsonian's National Museum of American History, known for high standards of accuracy, was selling a commemorative book about Mr. Trump riddled with questionable notions, such as that Hillary Clinton deserved more blame than Mr. Trump did for the so-called birther campaign questioning Mr. Obama's citizenship. (After that report, the museum said it was removing the book pending an investigation into whether it met standards for accuracy.)

The administration's decision to eradicate nearly any reference to "climate change" on the White House website could be expected given Mr. Trump's promises to overturn his predecessors' climate policies. But it set off concerns among climate scientists that it would extend to valuable government data — fears that also apply to the sanctity of other administration-controlled data. (Mr. Fleischer, for one, noted that career bureaucrats would blow the whistle on any moves to manipulate government data.)

Then there is the central information center of any White House: the pressroom.

On Thursday, Jim Hoft, the founder of The Gateway Pundit, said the White House was giving his site an official press credential. The Gateway Pundit promoted hoaxes such as one alleging that protesters in Austin, Tex., were bused in by the liberal donor George Soros. (The originator of that story told The New York Times that his assertions were not supported by fact.)

The White House has not confirmed that it will credential Gateway Pundit, but Mr. Hoft's announcement stoked anxiety among traditional reporters that the new administration will pack the pressroom with sympathetic organizations willing to promote falsehoods — or, perhaps, "alternative facts." It's one thing if that creates a false feedback loop about the size of an inauguration crowd — and quite another if it does so about a more important national security matter, as the CNN chief national security correspondent, Jim Sciutto, said over the weekend.

Mr. McClellan, the Bush press secretary, warned in an interview with me on Sunday that Mr. Spicer might come to regret it if reporters started to doubt the veracity of what he told them.

"There will be tough times ahead — there are for every White House — and that's when that credibility and trust is most important," Mr. McClellan said. But more important, he said, when you're at the White House lectern, "you're speaking for the free world to some extent, and what ideals are you holding up for that free world?"

There's nothing exceptional about the ones that aren't true.

The President Versus 'Fake News,' Again

OPINION | BY BRET STEPHENS | JUNE 29, 2017

OF THOSE FROM WHOM little is expected, much is forgiven. And of those from whom much is expected, little is forgiven. Such are the standards by which Donald Trump's deliberate assaults on the news media need to be understood and feared.

I write this following Trump's latest tirades against the Fourth Estate, including an early morning tweet on Tuesday denouncing "Fake News CNN" for having been "caught falsely pushing their phony Russian stories." That was followed 17 minutes later by a larger eruption, in which the president named NBC, CBS, ABC, The Washington Post and this newspaper as "all Fake News!"

And in case the message didn't penetrate, the deputy press secretary, Sarah Huckabee Sanders, denounced the "constant barrage of fake news" from CNN and touted a video in which conservative provocateur James O'Keefe secretly filmed a CNN producer (responsible for health stories), suggesting that the network's Russia coverage was ratings-driven.

"Whether it's accurate or not, I don't know," Ms. Sanders added about the video, lest there be any doubt about the White House's standards for accuracy.

CNN's sin is to have published a story, based on anonymous sourcing, which alleged that New York financier and Trump ally Anthony Scaramucci had ties to a Russian investment fund supposedly under investigation by the Senate.

The story failed to undergo CNN's usual vetting procedures and was later retracted. For good measure, the three journalists behind the story resigned and the network apologized to Scaramucci, who was gracious in accepting it.

As for this White House, graciousness becomes it about as well as napalm becomes an igloo. And the president must have been relieved to have something to do with his thumbs other than twiddle them, as Mitch McConnell struggled to get a Republican majority for the Senate's health bill.

Yet before dismissing Trump's rants as evidence of his mental state, it's worth taking them seriously as proof of political acumen. On Monday, Gallup released its latest annual survey on confidence in institutions: It found that confidence in the presidency had fallen since last summer, to 32 percent from 36 percent.

That may be bad news for Trump, but it compares well against the 24 percent confidence level in TV news and 27 percent newspapers (though both are a bit up over a year ago). Among Republicans, just 14 percent of respondents had confidence in TV news, and just 12 percent in newspapers, but 60 percent had confidence in the presidency.

If nothing else, Trump has the bully's cunning to pick on a target more unpopular than he is. And like a bully, he knows that his mark suffers the additional weakness of being susceptible to moral reproach. Institutions with a conscience have a tendency to be weak. They set standards to which they are bound to fall short, and publicly hold themselves to account.

Preserving — even cultivating — a capacity for shame, they are easily shamed. The shameless, having none, are only too glad to participate in the shaming.

That's why it was a mistake of CNN to let the three journalists — veteran reporter Thomas Frank and editors Lex Haris and Eric Lichtblau — responsible for the Scaramucci story go. The political success of Trump's assault on the press depends on his conflation of mistakes with dishonesty, of fallibility with fakery.

Assuming no dishonesties were involved in CNN's actions, cashiering the journalists does less to uphold the network's reputation for probity than it does to advance Trump's work. No news organization is going to pass an infallibility test, and advancing a perception that we should pass such a test merely sets us up for diminishing public regard. Journalistic honesty is better measured through corrections than dismissals.

That's a lesson that bears repeating now, as the White House's media vilification strategy comes to resemble a war on truth itself. I've noted elsewhere that Trump's notion of truth is whatever he can get away with, at any given moment, for any given purpose.

No serious news organization can stand for it, which is why this president and the press would be destined for an adversarial relationship even if their ideological leanings were more in sync. Call it the clash of epistemologies — truth as a construct of facts versus truth as a collection of wants and wishes. And never the twain shall meet.

In the meantime, the news media ought to take care not to underestimate the threat it faces from this White House. We have set ourselves up as guardians of Truth, a hard job in any circumstance, made additionally difficult by our inevitable errors in judgment and reporting, by an earnestness often mistaken for arrogance, and by our conviction that we are owed answers to whatever questions we wish to ask.

On the other side is a president who believes in none of this; who commands a following that believes in none of it; and who knows the power of holding the media accountable to its stringent standards and holding himself accountable only to his own.

How do you shame the shameless? You can't. But you can at least deny him the right to shame you. Something to consider over at CNN.

Wielding Claims of 'Fake News,' Conservatives Take Aim at Mainstream Media

BY JEREMY W. PETERS | DEC. 25, 2016

WASHINGTON — The C.I.A., the F.B.I. and the White House may all agree that Russia was behind the hacking that interfered with the election. But that was of no import to the website Breitbart News, which dismissed reports on the intelligence assessment as "left-wing fake news."

Rush Limbaugh has diagnosed a more fundamental problem. "The fake news is the everyday news" in the mainstream media, he said on his radio show recently. "They just make it up." Some supporters of President-elect Donald J. Trump have also taken up the call. As reporters were walking out of a Trump rally this month in Orlando, Fla., a man heckled them with shouts of "Fake news!"

Until now, that term had been widely understood to refer to fabricated news accounts that are meant to spread virally online. But conservative cable and radio personalities, top Republicans and even Mr. Trump himself, incredulous about suggestions that fake stories may have helped swing the election, have appropriated the term and turned it against any news they see as hostile to their agenda.

In defining "fake news" so broadly and seeking to dilute its meaning, they are capitalizing on the declining credibility of all purveyors of information, one product of the country's increasing political polarization. And conservatives, seeing an opening to undermine the mainstream media, a longtime foe, are more than happy to dig the hole deeper.

"Over the years, we've effectively brainwashed the core of our audience to distrust anything that they disagree with. And now it's gone too far," said John Ziegler, a conservative radio host, who has been critical of what he sees as excessive partisanship by pundits. "Because the gatekeepers have lost all credibility in the minds of consumers, I don't see how you reverse it."

Journalists who work to separate fact from fiction see a dangerous conflation of stories that turn out to be wrong because of a legitimate misunderstanding with those whose clear intention is to deceive. A report, shared more than a million times on social media, that the pope had endorsed Mr. Trump was undeniably false. But was it "fake news" to report on data models that showed Hillary Clinton with overwhelming odds of winning the presidency? Are opinion articles fake if they cherry-pick facts to draw disputable conclusions?

"Fake news was a term specifically about people who purposely fabricated stories for clicks and revenue," said David Mikkelson, the founder of Snopes, the myth-busting website. "Now it includes bad reporting, slanted journalism and outright propaganda. And I think we're doing a disservice to lump all those things together."

The right's labeling of "fake news" evokes one of the most successful efforts by conservatives to reorient how Americans think about news media objectivity: the move by Fox News to brand its conservative-slanted coverage as "fair and balanced." Traditionally, mainstream media outlets had thought of their own approach in those terms, viewing their coverage as strictly down the middle. Republicans often found that laughable.

As with Fox's ubiquitous promotion of its slogan, conservatives' appropriation of the "fake news" label is an effort to further erode the mainstream media's claim to be a reliable and accurate source.

"What I think is so unsettling about the fake news cries now is that their audience has already sort of bought into this idea that journalism has no credibility or legitimacy," said Angelo Carusone, the president of Media Matters, a liberal group that polices the news media for bias. "Therefore, by applying that term to credible outlets, it becomes much more believable."

Conservative news media are now awash in the "fake news" condemnations. When coverage of Mr. Trump's choice for labor secretary, Andrew F. Puzder, highlighted his opposition to minimum wage increases, the writer and radio host Erick Erickson wrote that Mr. Puzder should have been getting more credit for pointing out that such increases lead to higher unemployment. "To say otherwise is to push fake news," he wrote. (The effects actually have been found to vary from city to city.)

Infowars, the website run by the conservative provocateur and conspiracy theorist Alex Jones, labeled as "fake news" a CNN report that Ivanka Trump would move into the office in the White House normally reserved for the first lady.

Mr. Trump has used the term to deny news reports, as he did on Twitter recently after various outlets said he would stay on as the executive producer of "The New Celebrity Apprentice" after taking office in January. "Ridiculous & untrue — FAKE NEWS!" he wrote. (He will be credited as executive producer, a spokesman for the show's creator, Mark Burnett, has said. But it is unclear what work, if any, he will do on the show.)

Many conservatives are pushing back at the outrage over fake news because they believe that liberals, unwilling to accept Mr. Trump's victory, are attributing his triumph to nefarious external factors.

"The left refuses to admit that the fundamental problem isn't the Russians or Jim Comey or 'fake news' or the Electoral College," said Laura Ingraham, the author and radio host. "'Fake news' is just another fake excuse for their failed agenda."

Others see a larger effort to slander the basic journalistic function of fact-checking. Nonpartisan websites like Snopes and FactCheck.org have found themselves maligned when they have disproved stories that had been flattering to conservatives.

When Snopes wrote about a State Farm insurance agent in Louisiana who had posted a sign outside his office that likened taxpayers who voted for President Obama to chickens supporting Colonel Sanders, Mr. Mikkelson, the site's founder, was smeared as a partisan Democrat who had never bothered to reach out to the agent for comment. Neither is true.

"They're trying to float anything they can find out there to discredit fact-checking," he said.

There are already efforts by highly partisan conservatives to claim that their fact-checking efforts are the same as those of independent outlets like Snopes, which employ research teams to dig into seemingly dubious claims.

Sean Hannity, the Fox News host, has aired "fact-checking" segments on his program. Michelle Malkin, the conservative columnist, has a web program, "Michelle Malkin Investigates," in which she conducts her own investigative reporting.

The market in these divided times is undeniably ripe. "We now live in this fragmented media world where you can block people you disagree with. You can only be exposed to stories that make you feel good about what you want to believe," Mr. Ziegler, the radio host, said. "Unfortunately, the truth is unpopular a lot. And a good fairy tale beats a harsh truth every time."

Trump Hands Out 'Fake News Awards,' Sans the Red Carpet

BY MATT FLEGENHEIMER AND MICHAEL M. GRYNBAUM | JAN. 17, 2018

WASHINGTON — President Trump — who gleefully questioned President Barack Obama's birthplace for years without evidence, long insisted on the guilt of the Central Park Five despite exonerating proof and claimed that millions of illegal ballots cost him the popular vote in 2016 — wanted to have a word with the American public about accuracy in reporting.

On Wednesday, after weeks of shifting deadlines, and cryptic clues, Mr. Trump released his long-promised "Fake News Awards," an anti-media project that had alarmed advocates of press freedom and heartened his political base.

"And the FAKE NEWS winners are ...," he wrote on Twitter at 8 p.m.

The message linked, at first, to a malfunctioning page on GOP.com, the Republican National Committee website. An error screen read: "The site is temporarily offline, we are working to bring it back up. Please try back later."

When the page came back online less than an hour later, it resembled a Republican Party news release. Headlined "The Highly Anticipated 2017 Fake News Awards" and attributed to "Team GOP," it included a list of Trump administration accomplishments and jabs at news organizations presented in the form of an 11-point list.

The "winners" were CNN, mentioned four times; The New York Times, with two mentions; and ABC, The Washington Post, Time and Newsweek, with one mention apiece.

Taken as a whole, Mr. Trump's examples of grievances came as no surprise to anyone who has read his complaints about the media on Twitter.

The various reports singled out by Mr. Trump touched on serious issues, like the media's handling of the investigation by the special

DOUG MILLS/THE NEW YORK TIMES

Sarah Huckabee Sanders, the White House press secretary, on Wednesday, hours before the awards were announced. "I know you're all waiting to see if you are big winners, I'm sure," she told reporters.

counsel Robert S. Mueller III into the Trump campaign's possible ties to Russia, and frivolous matters, like the manner in which journalists conveyed how the president fed fish during a stop at a koi pond on his visit to Japan.

The first item on the list referred not to a news article but to a short opinion piece posted on The Times's website at 12:42 on the night Mr. Trump became president: "The New York Times' Paul Krugman claimed on the day of President Trump's historic, landslide victory that the economy will 'never' recover," the entry read.

What Mr. Krugman actually wrote was this: "If the question is when markets will recover, a first-pass answer is never." Mr. Krugman concluded his election night take by predicting that a global recession was likely, while adding the caveat, "I suppose we could get lucky somehow."

Three days later, Mr. Krugman retracted his prediction of an economic collapse, saying he overreacted.

The next target was Brian Ross of ABC News, who was suspended by the network last month because of an erroneous report.

ABC apologized for and corrected Mr. Ross's report that Michael T. Flynn, the former national security adviser, planned to testify that Mr. Trump had directed him to make contact with Russian officials when Mr. Trump was still a candidate.

In fact, Mr. Trump had directed Mr. Flynn to make contact after the election, when he was president-elect.

At the time of Mr. Ross's suspension, Kathleen Culver, the director of the Center for Journalism Ethics at the University of Wisconsin-Madison, said that the president was likely to use the mistake as ammunition against his political opponents — an observation that seemed borne out by the "Fake News Awards."

The third entry on the GOP.com list went after CNN, a favorite target of the president, for reporting incorrectly last month that the president's eldest child, Donald Trump Jr., had received advance notice from WikiLeaks about a trove of hacked documents that it planned to release during last year's presidential campaign.

In fact, the email to the younger Mr. Trump was sent a day after the documents, stolen from the Democratic National Committee, were made available to the general public. The correction undercut the main thrust of CNN's story, which had been seized on by critics of the president as evidence of coordination between WikiLeaks and the Trump campaign.

Another entry on the list took on The Washington Post, claiming that it had "FALSELY reported the President's massive sold-out rally in Pensacola, Florida, was empty. Dishonest reporter showed picture of empty arena HOURS before crowd started pouring in."

The reporter in question was David Weigel, who had posted the photo in question on his Twitter account before quickly deleting it. The Post itself did not publish the photo or a report on the size of the crowd at the Trump event. The "Fake News Awards" entry, however, conflated a reporter's tweet with the publication itself. It also omitted the fact that Mr. Weigel deleted his tweet and apologized for it when it was pointed out to him that it was misleading. Further, it did not mention that Mr. Trump had called for Mr. Weigel to be fired over the tweet. (He was not.)

The content of the 11-point list was perhaps less notable than its premise: a sitting president using his bully pulpit for a semi-formalized attack on the free press.

In two subsequent tweets on Wednesday night, Mr. Trump added that there were "many great reporters I respect" and defended his administration's record in the face of "a very biased media."

The technical anticlimax seemed a fitting end to a peculiar saga that began in November when Mr. Trump floated the bestowing of a "FAKE NEWS TROPHY."

The idea matured into the "Fake News Awards," which the president initially said in a Jan. 2 Twitter post he would give out on Jan. 8 to honor "the most corrupt & biased of the Mainstream Media."

With the date approaching, Mr. Trump wrote on Twitter that the event would be moved to Wednesday because "the interest in, and importance of, these awards is far greater than anyone could have anticipated!"

From the beginning, the awards were the sort of Trumpian production that seemed easy to mock but difficult to ignore. Members of the news media joked about the speeches they would prepare, the tuxedos and gowns they would fetch. It would be an honor, they said, just to be nominated.

Here, it seemed, was the opéra bouffe climax of Mr. Trump's campaign against the media, a bizarro-world spectacle that both encapsulated and parodied the president's animus toward a major democratic institution.

Late-night comedy shows created satirical Emmys-style advertising campaigns to snag what some referred to as a coveted "Fakey."

"The Late Show With Stephen Colbert" bought a billboard in Times Square, nominating itself in categories like "Least Breitbarty" and

"Corruptest Fakeness." Jimmy Kimmel, who has emerged as a Trump bête noire, called it "the Stupid People's Choice Awards."

Politico reported that the awards could even pose an ethical issue for White House aides, with some experts arguing that the event would breach a ban on government officials using their office to explicitly promote or deride private organizations.

And press advocates cringed at the prospect of a gala dedicated to the phrase "fake news," which has already helped corrode trust in journalism in the United States and around the world. In response to Mr. Trump's endeavor, the Committee to Protect Journalists this month recognized the president among the "world leaders who have gone out of their way to attack the press and undermine the norms that support freedom of the media."

Two Republicans from Arizona, Senator John McCain and Senator Jeff Flake, denounced Mr. Trump's anti-press attacks, with Mr. Flake noting in a speech on the Senate floor on Wednesday that the president had borrowed a term from Stalin to describe the media: "enemy of the people."

The buzz around the president's latest anti-press stunt has contributed to a larger shift in American attitudes toward the press.

In a study released this week by Gallup and the Knight Foundation, 66 percent of Americans who were surveyed said most news organizations blurred opinion and fact, up from 42 percent in 1984. "Fake news" was deemed a threat to democracy by a majority of respondents.

Mr. Trump's list did not mention BuzzFeed, a media outlet that drew his ire last year when it published a salacious and largely unsubstantiated intelligence dossier that purported to lay out how Russia had aided the Trump campaign. On Jan. 8, President Trump's longtime lawyer, Michael D. Cohen, filed a defamation lawsuit in federal court against Fusion GPS, the firm behind the report, as well as a separate lawsuit against BuzzFeed in state court.

Mr. Trump also did not mention Michael Wolff, the author of the slashing, if error-specked, best seller, "Fire and Fury: Inside the

Trump White House," although a lawyer working on his behalf had sent a letter demanding that the publisher Henry Holt and Company halt publication of the book.

"Fire and Fury" did not come out until Jan. 5, so perhaps the author will receive a prominent mention next January, if the president sees fit to give out the 2018 Fake News Awards.

Am I Imagining This?

OPINION | BY ROGER COHEN | FEB. 10, 2017

FACT-BASED JOURNALISM is a ridiculous, tautological phrase. It's like talking about oxygen-based human life. There is no other kind. Facts are journalism's foundation; the pursuit of them, without fear or favor, is its main objective.

But in this time of President Trump's almost daily "fake news" accusations against The New York Times, and of his counselor Kellyanne Conway's "alternative facts," and of untruths seeping like a plague from the highest office in the land, there's increasing talk of "real" or "fact-based" journalism.

That's ominous. Fact-based as opposed to what other type? To state the obvious, fake news websites fed by kids in Macedonia to make a buck are not journalism. These sites use fabricated stuff in journalism's garb to further political ends.

There's a targeted "Gaslight" attack on journalists designed to make them doubt their sanity. It's emanating from the White House and aims to drag everyone down the rabbit hole where 2+2=5.

Velocity trumps veracity. That is the puzzle and the menace of our age.

Speed and disruption have more psychological impact than truth and science. They shape the discourse. The debunking of a fake news story is seldom as powerful as the story itself. Trump says "X." Uproar! Hordes of journalists scurry to disprove "X." He moves on, never to mention it again, or claims that he did not say it, or insists that what he really said was "Y."

People begin to wonder: Am I imagining this? They feel that some infernal mechanism has taken hold and is dragging them toward an abyss. The president is a reference point; if he lies, lying seeps deep into the culture. Americans start to ask: Will we ever be able to dislodge these people from power? What are they capable of?

Simon Schama, the British historian, recently tweeted: "Indifference about the distinction between truth and lies is the precondition of fascism. When truth perishes so does freedom."

The enormity of the defiling of the White House in just three weeks is staggering. For decades the world's security was undergirded by America's word. The words that issued from the Oval Office were solemn. It was on America's word, as expressed by the president, that the European continent and allies like Japan built their postwar security.

Now the words that fall from Trump's pursed lips or, often misspelled, onto his Twitter feed are trite or false or meaningless. He's angry with Nordstrom, for heaven's sake, because the department store chain dropped his daughter Ivanka's clothing line! This is the concern of the leader of the free world.

Unpresidented!

I was struck by how Paul Horner, who runs a big Facebook fake-news operation, described our times in The Washington Post: "Honestly people are definitely dumber. They just keep passing stuff around. Nobody fact-checks anything anymore — I mean, that's how Trump got elected. He just said whatever he wanted, and people believed everything, and when the things he said turned out not to be true, people didn't care because they'd already accepted it. It's real scary. I've never seen anything like it."

We've never seen anything like it because when hundreds of millions of Americans are connected, anyone, clueless or not, can disseminate what they like with a click.

Horner came up, during the campaign, with the fake news story that a protester at a Trump rally had been paid $3,500. It went viral. We've had fake news accounts of how Hillary Clinton paid $62 million to Beyoncé and Jay Z to perform in Cleveland, and how Khizr Khan, the father of the Muslim American officer killed in Iraq, was an agent of the Muslim Brotherhood. Fake news — BREAKING! SHOCKING! — swayed the election.

Now we have President Trump suggesting that the real fake news is his negative polls — along with CNN, The New York Times, The Washington Post and any other news organizations that are doing their jobs: holding his authority to account and bearing witness to his acts. Stephen Bannon, Trump's man of the shadows, thinks the media should "keep its mouth shut." We won't.

Sometimes I try to imagine what Trump's Reichstag fire moment might be. In February 1933, a few weeks after Hitler became chancellor, fire engulfed the parliament in Berlin — an act of arson whose origin is still unclear. A recent New Yorker article by George Prochnik quoted the Austrian writer Stefan Zweig on Hitler's savage reaction: "At one blow all of justice in Germany was smashed."

From a president who loathes the press, who insults the judiciary, who has no time for American ideals of liberty or democracy, and whose predilection for violence is evident, what would be the reaction to a Reichstag fire in American guise — say a major act of terrorism?

We can only shudder at the thought.

Facts matter. The federal judiciary is pushing back. The administration is leaking. Journalism (no qualifier needed) has never been more important. Truth has not yet perished, but to deny that it is under siege would be to invite disaster.

The Age of Post-Truth Politics

BY WILLIAM DAVIES | AUG. 24, 2016

FACTS HOLD A SACRED place in Western liberal democracies. Whenever democracy seems to be going awry, when voters are manipulated or politicians are ducking questions, we turn to facts for salvation.

But they seem to be losing their ability to support consensus. PolitiFact has found that about 70 percent of Donald Trump's "factual" statements actually fall into the categories of "mostly false," "false" and "pants on fire" untruth.

For the Brexit referendum, Leave argued that European Union membership costs Britain 350 million pounds a week, but failed to account for the money received in return.

The sense is widespread: We have entered an age of post-truth politics.

As politics becomes more adversarial and dominated by television performances, the status of facts in public debate rises too high. We place expectations on statistics and expert testimony that strains them to breaking point. Rather than sit coolly outside the fray of political argument, facts are now one of the main rhetorical weapons within it.

How can we still be speaking of "facts" when they no longer provide us with a reality that we all agree on? The problem is that the experts and agencies involved in producing facts have multiplied, and many are now for hire. If you really want to find an expert willing to endorse a fact, and have sufficient money or political clout behind you, you probably can.

The combination of populist movements with social media is often held responsible for post-truth politics. Individuals have growing opportunities to shape their media consumption around their own opinions and prejudices, and populist leaders are ready to encourage them.

But to focus on recent, more egregious abuses of facts is to overlook the ways in which the authority of facts has been in decline

ANDREW TESTA FOR THE NEW YORK TIMES

People demonstrated in London against Brexit in July.

for quite some time. Newspapers might provide resistance to the excesses of populist demagogy, but not to the broader crisis of facts.

The problem is the oversupply of facts in the 21st century: There are too many sources, too many methods, with varying levels of credibility, depending on who funded a given study and how the eye-catching number was selected.

According to the cultural historian Mary Poovey, the tendency to represent society in terms of facts first arose in late medieval times with the birth of accounting. What was new about merchant bookkeeping, Dr. Poovey argued, was that it presented a type of truth that could apparently stand alone, without requiring any interpretation or faith on the part of the person reading it.

In the centuries that followed, accounting was joined by statistics, economics, surveys and a range of other numerical methods. But even as these methods expanded, they tended to be the preserve of small, tight-knit institutions, academic societies and professional associations who could uphold standards. National statistical associations, for example, soon provided the know-how for official statistics offices, affiliated with and funded by governments.

In the 20th century, an industry for facts emerged. Market-research companies began to conduct surveys in the 1920s and extended into opinion polling in the 1930s. Think tanks like the American Enterprise Institute were established during and after World War II to apply statistics and economics to the design of new government policies, typically in the service of one political agenda or another. The idea of "evidence-based policy," popular among liberal politicians in the late 1990s and early 2000s, saw economics being heavily leaned on to justify government programs, in an allegedly post-ideological age.

Of course the term "fact" isn't reserved exclusively for numbers. But it does imply a type of knowledge that can be reliably parceled out in public, without constant need for verification or interpretation.

Yet there is one much more radical contributor to our post-truth politics that could ultimately be as transformative of our society as accounting proved to be 500 years ago.

We are in the middle of a transition from a society of facts to a society of data. During this interim, confusion abounds surrounding the exact status of knowledge and numbers in public life, exacerbating the sense that truth itself is being abandoned.

The place to start in understanding this transition is with the spread of "smart" technologies into everyday life, sometimes called the "internet of things." Thanks to the presence of smartphones and smartcards in our pockets, the dramatic uptake of social media, the rise of e-commerce as a means of purchasing goods and services, and the spread of sensory devices across public spaces, we leave a vast quantity of data in our wake as we go about our daily activities.

Like statistics or other traditional facts, this data is quantitative in nature. What's new is both its unprecedented volume (the "big" in big data) and also the fact that it is being constantly collected by default, rather than by deliberate expert design. Numbers are being generated much faster than we have any specific use for. But they can nevertheless be mined to get a sense of how people are behaving and what they are thinking.

The promise of facts is to settle arguments between warring perspectives and simplify the issues at stake. For instance, politicians might disagree over the right economic policy, but if they can agree that "the economy has grown by 2 percent" and "unemployment is 5 percent," then there is at least a shared stable reality that they can argue over.

The promise of data, by contrast, is to sense shifts in public sentiment. By analyzing Twitter using algorithms, for example, it is possible to get virtually real-time updates on how a given politician is perceived. This is what's known as "sentiment analysis."

There are precedents for this, such as the "worm" that monitors live audience reaction during a televised presidential debate, rising and falling in response to each moment of a candidate's rhetoric. Financial markets represent the sentiments of traders as they fluctuate throughout the day. Stock markets never produce a fact as to what Cisco is worth in the way that an accountant can; they provide a window into how thousands of people around the world are feeling about Cisco, from one minute to the next.

Journalists and politicians can no more ignore a constant audit of collective mood than C.E.O.s can ignore the fluctuations in their companies' share prices. If the British government had spent more time trying to track public sentiment toward the European Union and less time repeating the facts of how the British economy benefited from membership in the union, it might have fought the Brexit referendum campaign differently and more successfully.

Dominic Cummings, one of the leading pro-Brexit campaigners, mocked what he called outdated polling techniques. He also asked one pollster to add a question on "enthusiasm," and, employing scientists to mine very large, up-to-the-minute data sets, to gauge voter mood and to react accordingly with ads and voter-turnout volunteers.

It is possible to live in a world of data but no facts. Think of how we employ weather forecasts: We understand that it is not a fact that it will be 75 degrees on Thursday, and that figure will fluctuate all the time. Weather forecasting works in a similar way to sentiment analysis, bringing data from a wide range of sensory devices, and converting this into a constantly evolving narrative about the near future.

However, this produces some chilling possibilities for politics. Once numbers are viewed more as indicators of current sentiment, rather than as statements about reality, how are we to achieve any consensus on the nature of social, economic and environmental problems, never mind agree on the solutions?

Conspiracy theories prosper under such conditions. And while we will have far greater means of knowing how many people believe those theories, we will have far fewer means of persuading them to abandon them.

CHAPTER 5

Fake News Around the World

The United States under the Trump administration is not the only society grappling with the effects of fake news. A wave of recent elections around the world were in danger of being undermined, and the United States' own foreign policy has been influenced by fake news. "News" is no longer primarily a local phenomenon. It is global, not only in scope, but also in its production and consumption. "News" is produced all over the world, and fake news from Moscow or Massachusetts can rattle a politician in Peru or an electorate in Ethiopia.

The C.I.A.'s Fake News Campaign

BY KENNETH OSGOOD | OCT. 13, 2017

RUSSIA'S CRAFTY CAMPAIGN to hack the 2016 election may seem unprecedented, but in a way it's not. Sure, secret agents and front groups have hacked email systems, dumped documents on WikiLeaks, paid an army of internet trolls and spent thousands buying political ads on social media. It all seems new because the technologies are new. But it's not the first time a government tried to mess with our heads by manipulating our media.

In fact, for more than two decades during the Cold War, the public was bombarded by an enormous publicity campaign to shape American views of Russia and its foreign policy. Advertisements appeared on every TV network, on radio stations across the country and in hundreds of newspapers. The campaign may have been the largest and most consistent source of political advertising in American history. And it was orchestrated by a big, powerful intelligence service: the Central Intelligence Agency.

It all began as a cover story. As the Cold War was getting underway, the C.I.A. wanted to take the fight into Russia's backyard. So, in 1950, it created Radio Free Europe, a government-sponsored broadcasting station. Ostensibly, it provided unbiased news for Eastern Europeans, but in fact the agency used it to wage a subversive campaign to weaken Communist governments behind the Iron Curtain.

But how to hide the agency's hand? How to account for the millions of C.I.A. dollars pouring into the broadcasting station? Simple: pretend that ordinary Americans are paying the bills.

The C.I.A.'s freewheeling spymaster, Frank Wisner, created a well-heeled and well-connected front group, the National Committee for a Free Europe. Each year it ran an enormous fund-raising campaign called the Crusade for Freedom (later renamed the Radio Free Europe Fund) that implored Americans to donate "freedom dollars" to combat Kremlin lies, complete with annual appeals resembling a hybrid of World War II war bond campaigns and contemporary NPR pledge drives.

Every president from Harry Truman to Richard Nixon endorsed the campaign. So did hundreds of governors, mayors, celebrities, editors and executives. Entertainers like Ronald Reagan, Rock Hudson, Jerry Lewis and the Kingston Trio pleaded for donations on radio and television. The Hollywood producers Darryl Zanuck and Cecil B. DeMille amplified those messages, as did powerful media figures like Bill Paley, the president of CBS; C. D. Jackson, the publisher of Fortune; and the media mogul Henry Luce. Even newspaper delivery boys played a part, soliciting donations from subscribers on their paper routes.

Then there was the Ad Council, the same industry organization that turned Smokey Bear into a cultural icon. The council sponsored the crusade as a public service, arranging for broadcasters to run ads without charge. The Ad Council's sponsorship translated into as much as $2 billion worth of free advertising over the campaign's history, in 2017 dollars.

The message was simple: Russia was aggressive; Communism was awful. The enemy couldn't be trusted. Typical ads conveyed a brutalized vision of life behind the Iron Curtain: "a strip of Communist-controlled hell-on-earth," one read. Donating a few bucks would save Czechs, Poles, Hungarians and others from this tyranny. Many thousands of Americans took the bait. They dutifully wrote checks to Radio Free Europe, and their contributions were magnified by gifts from many of the country's biggest corporations, yielding, on average, about $1 million annually.

It wasn't enough: The donations barely covered the cost of running the "fund-raising drives," to say nothing of Radio Free Europe's $30 million annual budgets. But that wasn't the point.

Declassified documents reveal that almost from the start, the C.I.A. saw that it could exploit the fund-raising campaign as a conduit for domestic propaganda. It was a way to rally public support for the Cold War by dramatizing Communist repression and stoking fears of a worldwide menace. The plight of Eastern Europe brought moral clarity to the Cold War, and it cemented the region as a vital national interest in American domestic politics.

Its impact outlived the campaign itself. Even though the pleas for donations ended in 1971, when the C.I.A. was exposed and stopped funding the station, they cemented anti-Communist hostility that animated conservative opposition to détente in the 1970s. It provided the leitmotif for Reagan's denunciations of the "evil empire" in the 1980s. One can even hear echoes in Donald Trump's recent speech to the United Nations: His long digression on the evils of socialism seems drawn from the heated rhetoric of ads gone by.

So, too, does our post-truth media environment carry voices from this past. The crusade blasted all information from enemy sources as lies and deceit — fake news, we could say. This counter-propaganda sought to inoculate the public from being receptive to anything said by the other side. It's a tactic we've seen play out in real time on the president's Twitter feed.

And almost certainly, Radio Free Europe itself — which continues to operate out of its headquarters in Prague — has shaped Vladimir Putin's worldview. Russia has long tried to claim Eastern Europe as its sphere of influence. Moscow hated the station for its meddling. As a K.G.B. officer, Mr. Putin no doubt spent many hours fretting over its activities in the Soviet bloc. It was a major irritant. He may even see the 2016 election hack as a way to even the score. If so, it's payback indeed.

‘Fake News,’ Trump’s Obsession, Is Now a Cudgel for Strongmen

BY STEVEN ERLANGER | DEC. 12, 2017

BRUSSELS — President Trump routinely invokes the phrase “fake news” as a rhetorical tool to undermine opponents, rally his political base and try to discredit a mainstream American media that is aggressively investigating his presidency.

But he isn’t the only leader enamored with the phrase. Following Mr. Trump’s example, many of the world’s autocrats and dictators are taking a shine to it, too.

When Amnesty International released a report about prison deaths in Syria, the Syrian president, Bashar al-Assad, retorted that “we are living in a fake-news era.” President Nicolás Maduro of Venezuela, who is steadily rolling back democracy in his country, blamed the global media for “lots of false versions, lots of lies,” saying “this is what we call ‘fake news’ today.”

In Myanmar, where international observers accuse the military of conducting a genocidal campaign against the Rohingya Muslims, a security official told The New York Times that “there is no such thing as Rohingya,” adding: “It is fake news.” In Russia, a Foreign Ministry spokeswoman, Maria Zakharova, told a CNN reporter to “stop spreading lies and fake news.” Her ministry now uses a big red stamp, “FAKE,” on its website to label news stories it dislikes.

Around the world, authoritarians, populists and other political leaders have seized on the phrase “fake news” — and the legitimacy conferred upon it by an American president — as a tool for attacking their critics and, in some cases, deliberately undermining the institutions of democracy. In countries where press freedom is restricted or under considerable threat — including Russia, China, Turkey, Libya, Poland, Hungary, Thailand, Somalia and others — political leaders have invoked “fake news” as justification for beating back media scrutiny.

ADAM DEAN FOR THE NEW YORK TIMES

Rohingya refugees after crossing the Naf River that separates Myanmar and Bangladesh. A Myanmar security official told The New York Times, "There is no such thing as Rohingya," adding, "It is fake news."

Just this week, the official newspaper of the Chinese Communist Party, People's Daily, used Mr. Trump's words to undercut critical media coverage of an increasingly authoritarian Beijing.

"If the president of the United States claims that his nation's leading media outlets are a stain on America," the paper wrote, "then negative news about China and other countries should be taken with a grain of salt, since it is likely that bias and political agendas are distorting the real picture."

Not quite a year into his presidency, Mr. Trump has shaken the global status quo, with his "America First" ethos, his disdain for global trade and multilateral treaties, and his testy relationships with many traditional allies (and seemingly warm embrace of many traditional rivals). But the president's mantra of "fake news" stirs different concerns among many foreign politicians and analysts, who fear it erodes public confidence in democratic institutions at a

DOUG MILLS/THE NEW YORK TIMES

President Trump with President Rodrigo Duterte of the Philippines at the 31st Asean summit meeting in Manila last month.

time when populism and authoritarianism are returning in many regions.

"Trump doesn't only talk about fake news, but attacks the media as fake news, and that's an attack on the free press," said Marietje Schaake, a Dutch member of the European Parliament who focuses on human rights and the digital landscape. "As the leader of a country that traditionally defends human rights, that's very serious, and of course it has a major impact worldwide."

Richard Javad Heydarian, a political scientist at De La Salle University in Manila and the author of a book on President Rodrigo Duterte of the Philippines, said that American soft power, long rooted in advocacy of democracy, was "in a state of total collapse," allowing strongman leaders like Mr. Duterte greater leeway to ignore democratic norms.

"With Trump in power, no one is talking about human rights, only fake news, and that's great for Duterte," he said. "They both see themselves as populists facing a conspiracy of liberal elites. They think they are victims of fake news."

Though the term "fake news" has been around at least since the 1890s, according to Merriam-Webster, Mr. Trump is most responsible for making it a big part of the current global conversation. Now it is so common that Collins Dictionary decided to make it this year's "word of the year," finding in early November that the use of the term had risen by 365 percent since 2016.

Helen Newstead, Collins's head of language content, said that " 'Fake news,' either as a statement of fact or as an accusation, has been inescapable this year, contributing to the undermining of society's trust in news reporting."

The problem, of course, is that fake news is a real problem, especially on social media. United States intelligence agencies have concluded that Russia used fake news reports as part of an effort to interfere in the 2016 presidential election on behalf of Mr. Trump. The presence of fake news in the globalized stream of media content helps blur the line with traditional, fact-based news.

How much the fake-news epithet has damaged journalism, however, is difficult to say, given the pre-existing difficulties of doing untrammeled reporting in countries where the media is already under the thumb of the state and where journalists have been murdered or imprisoned, not simply insulted or mocked. But there is little question that social media, with its huge reach and its vulnerability to bots and manipulation, has helped to amplify criticism from political leaders and undermine trust in traditional journalism.

"Trump has succeeded in building an alternative reality separate from the mainstream media's efforts at democratic, rational politics," said John Lloyd, a senior research fellow at the Reuters Institute for the Study of Journalism at the University of Oxford. "Of course journalists make mistakes, but those errors are amplified by the charge of 'fake news,' " he said. "The mainstream media is portrayed as the tool of an arrogant, out-of-touch elite, who use that tool to keep down the marginalized."

The fake-news narrative also complicates the work of democracy advocates in countries where democracy is already under assault. Kenneth Roth, the executive director of Human Rights Watch, said that "the sad irony is that Trump's greatest harm to human rights may not be his infatuation with abusive strongmen but his undermining of the fact-based discourse that is essential for reining them in."

He added: "In countries where the judicial system is unable or unwilling to enforce rights — most countries — the human rights movement's main tool is to investigate and publicize official misconduct. Autocrats go to great lengths to avoid that shaming, because it tends to delegitimize them before their public and their peers."

Some analysts say Mr. Trump's success at creating an alternative reality and disparaging an adversarial media both copies and augments the tactics of Russia's president, Vladimir V. Putin, noting that Mr. Putin's propagandists "create a barrage of fake facts" on politically sensitive topics such as the conflict in Ukraine in order to sow public cynicism and uncertainty. Russia and China also create "positive" fake news on social media to inspire patriotism at home.

"People accept these versions or are confused by them, unclear as to what is correct," said Mr. Lloyd, author of "The Power and the Story: The Global Battle for News and Information." "Putin above all has grasped this and uses it against his enemies. The concept of 'fake news' is used to tar any uncomfortable fact."

Other governments have also embraced the phrase, especially to attack media outlets that Mr. Trump constantly disparages. One glaring example came in Libya, after CNN aired video showing a migrant being auctioned as a slave. Libyan leaders responded by using Mr. Trump's attacks against CNN to try to cast doubt on the network's report.

Prime Minister Hun Sen of Cambodia, who was put in charge of the occupied country by the Vietnamese Army more than 30 years ago, shut down The Cambodia Daily and jailed journalists and recently banned the opposition party. Now he also has focused his attacks on

OMAR HAVANA FOR THE NEW YORK TIMES

Inside the newsroom of The Cambodia Daily in Phnom Penh in August. Prime Minister Hun Sen shut down the newspaper and jailed journalists; his government also banned the opposition party.

Western media for writing about issues from corruption and repression to sex trafficking. "I would like to send a message to the president that your attack on CNN is right," Mr. Hun Sen said in August. "American media is very bad."

Prime Minister Najib Razak of Malaysia, embroiled in a scandal in which billions of dollars disappeared from the state investment fund, repeatedly calls accusations against him "fake news," including what he called "a well-known foreign newspaper," presumably a reference to The Wall Street Journal, which has reported on the disappearance of the funds. Mr. Trump once called Mr. Najib his "favorite prime minister." He also has hailed his "great relationship" with Mr. Duterte, the Philippine president, who has blamed "fake news" for coverage of his war on drug traffickers, which has killed thousands of Filipinos, many without trial.

Many media organizations are now introducing features to verify facts for readers. In France, Le Monde's Décodex was launched in

January as part of the fact-checking section of its website. In Britain, the BBC is starting a project to help secondary school pupils to identify real news and filter out fake or false information.

But it is a different matter when the president of the United States is the source, Ms. Schaake said. "There is significant damage to the credibility of the United States as the defender of human rights and democratic principles, of which press freedom is one of the pillars," she said.

Fake News Jeans: Travesty or Sign of Our Era?

BY VANESSA FRIEDMAN | JAN. 10, 2018

SINCE LAST SUNDAY'S Golden Globes, the question of what to wear to the various awards shows has become even more fraught than usual. It's not just about a pretty dress anymore, but about solidarity, statement making and so on.

Luckily, however, a solution to at least one such conundrum is at hand. Though there is as yet no official ceremony or red carpet attached to President Trump's Fake News awards, scheduled to take place next Wednesday (after being postponed from Monday), anyone who suspects that he or she may be in the cross hairs, has a perfect potential outfit. Or at least part of one.

VALERIO MEZZANOTTI FOR THE NEW YORK TIMES

Dior's message T-shirt from the spring 2017 collection.

Topshop, the British retailer, has created a pair of jeans in semi-stretch denim, with a red stripe down the side blaring, "Fake News" over and over again in white block letters. They look rather like a nod to artwork by Barbara Kruger. Just imagine them with a tuxedo jacket and heels instead of the sweatshirts they are paired with on Topshop's website, and bingo!

"The term 'Fake News' became so ubiquitous last year that it was officially named the word of the year, so we thought we'd immortalize this of-the-moment phrase on a pair of our jeans," said Mo Riach, Topshop's head of design, by way of explanation.

("Fake News" was chosen as the word of the year for 2017 by both the Collins English Dictionary and the American Dialect Society, in case you were wondering.)

The jeans, which cost $90 and come in gently faded denim with a mid-rise and straight legs, were a trending product on the brand's website by Tuesday, with 30 percent of the sales originating in the United States. By Wednesday, they were sold out.

Still, not everyone was so thrilled with the idea.

Because the disintegration of truth, science, and journalism is so fashionable. Give me a break @Topshop

— Amanda goodfried (@AGoodfried) Jan. 7, 2018

This exploitation of anything remotely iconic or zeitgeist-ish by the fashion industry is so crude and so recurrent that I'm starting to regret not thinking about these things before they hit the market

— Homelandz (@Homelandz) Jan. 7, 2018

Then some commentators got a little snarky about upset liberals.

Presumably part of the issue is that Topshop, while known for its slogan items (it has sold an average of one slogan T-shirt a minute since September, according to a spokeswoman), is not really known for its political positions, so the jeans smack of bandwagoning as opposed to a call to arms during a sensitive cultural moment.

Whether you think the jeans are a travesty or a triumph, however, the truth is that clothes have always been a popular outlet for political positioning, and this is increasingly true in the Trump administration. Mr. Trump is, after all, a president who loves branding of all kinds, is obsessed with image and visual messaging, has an alliterative way with a nickname and whose occasionally garbled use of language (remember covfefe?) has become part of the national lexicon in a way that practically begs a coffee cup. The flurry has all picked up steam since the presidential campaign, which included fashion statement making and symbolism on both sides: women who dressed up in pantsuits or suffragist white to support Hillary Clinton, and Mr. Trump and his "Make America Great Again" red baseball cap. That particular accessory was adapted late last year by the entrepreneur Elon Musk, who created "Boring Company" black baseball caps to promote his Los Angeles tunnel-drilling initiative.

The fashion runways, too, have been full of messaging. There was Dior's "We Should All Be Feminists" T-shirt version of Chimamanda Ngozi Adichie's TED Talk and Prabal Gurung's all-slogan show finale, with models wearing multiple phrases on their shirts, including "I am an immigrant" and "We will not be silenced." During the Globes, Connie Britton wore a shirt with the message "Poverty is Sexist" embroidered across the torso. Last summer, Mrs. Clinton modeled a special T-shirt made to raise money for Planned Parenthood bearing a pointed quote from Mr. Trump that became a cause unto itself: "Nasty Woman."

All of which suggests that while we can whine all we want about the superficiality of addressing these issues via style, none of this is going away any time soon, and it will probably get more ... well, trendy. We've just moved on from tees and hats to pants. The whole wide wardrobe world is now up for word grabs! (How's that for a tongue twister?)

It's only a matter of time before some other clever denim company takes a page from Topshop's book and realizes that Mr. Trump has recently provided us with yet another gem of a phrase, a version of which is just bound for clothing: Very Stable Jeanius.

Can't you just see it?

For Pope Francis, Fake News Goes Back to the Garden of Eden

BY JASON HOROWITZ | JAN. 24, 2018

ROME — The serpent in the Garden of Eden hissed the first fake news to Eve and it all went downhill from there, Pope Francis wrote in a major document about the phenomenon of fake news released on Wednesday.

"We need to unmask what could be called the 'snake-tactics' used by those who disguise themselves in order to strike at any time and place," the pope wrote in a message ahead of what the church has designated as its World Day of Social Communications, in May.

Arguing that the "crafty" serpent's effective disinformation campaign to get Eve to eat from the tree of knowledge "began the tragic history of human sin," he added, "I would like to contribute to our shared commitment to stemming the spread of fake news."

Pope Francis has worn many hats since his election in 2013 — Vatican reformer; global advocate for refugees, the poor, and world peace; and, more recently, defender of bishops accused of covering up for pedophile priests.

But in a varyingly sophisticated, spiritual and questionable analysis of the fake news epidemic, the 81-year-old pontiff tried on the cap of contemporary media critic to address an issue that has wreaked havoc and undermined democracies from the United States to Europe and beyond.

In doing so, he offered a largely cleareyed assessment of the problem, its social impact, and the responsibility of social media giants and journalists. And he called on news consumers to break out of their comfortable echo chambers and cushy news feeds by seeking out different points of view.

But at times the pope also conflated fake news, which is politically or economically motivated disinformation, with an incremental and sensational style of journalism he dislikes — a muddying of the waters that many democracy advocates have worried is corrosive to a free press and to the ideal of an informed populace.

He also failed to mention the political leaders who have used the phrase to discredit journalists and to dismiss inconvenient reporting.

Betraying a somewhat antiquated view that separates dead-tree and digital outlets, the pope defined fake news as the spreading "online or in the traditional media" of disinformation that is intended to deceive and manipulate consumers for political and economic interests.

He observed that fake news is effective because, like the snake in the garden, it insidiously mimics real news, and is "captious" — pope for clickbait — meaning that it grabs people's attention by exploiting "emotions like anxiety, contempt, anger and frustration."

Francis identified social networks as the delivery systems for such fake news.

"Untrue stories can spread so quickly that even authoritative denials fail to contain the damage," he wrote, adding that those living virtual lives in like-minded silos allow disinformation to thrive and that the absence of opposing viewpoints turns people into "unwilling accomplices in spreading biased and baseless ideas."

Russian hackers took advantage of just such conditions in the 2016 American elections, sowing discord and attempting to sway the electorate through sophisticated influence campaigns. Francis steered clear of such real-world examples. Instead, he broadly identified greed as a key engine for the spread of fake news

"Fake news often goes viral, spreading so fast that it is hard to stop, not because of the sense of sharing that inspires the social media, but because it appeals to the insatiable greed so easily aroused in human beings," he wrote.

The results, he said, are soul-killing.

Turning to the "The Brothers Karamazov," he quoted Dostoyevsky: "People who lie to themselves and listen to their own lie come to such a pass that they cannot distinguish the truth within them, or around them, and so lose all respect for themselves and for others." This leads to the coarsening of society, Francis said.

To combat fake news, the pope called for personal efforts to unmask disinformation, but he also praised educational programs, regulatory efforts and social media companies' progress in verifying personal identities "concealed behind millions of digital profiles."

In recent years, the European Union and several European countries have established offices to combat fake news — this week, Britain became the latest. And fake news has emerged as a major theme in the Italian elections scheduled for March 4, and it is often discussed in the Italian news media that imbues the Vatican.

The speaker of the lower house of the Italian Parliament, Laura Boldrini, has backed a program in Italian public schools to teach children how to identify fake news. The government announced this month an online service through the country's postal police that would respond to, and assess, accusations of fake news.

Likewise, Matteo Renzi, the leader of Italy's governing Democratic Party, has pressed Facebook to monitor its platform for fake news. Facebook has said it would dispatch a task force to address the problem before the Italian election.

Globally, Facebook's more consequential contribution may be a major policy change announced this month: It plans to step back from its de facto role as the world's news publisher. In the United States, more lawmakers are interested in regulating social media giants as they do traditional television broadcasters.

But the pope argued that the most "radical antidote" to the scourge of fake news lies in "purification by the truth." In Christianity, he said, that means living the truth through faith in Jesus, who, he observed, said, "I am the truth" and "the truth will set you free."

Along those lines, he argued that the marshaling of undeniable facts to hurt and discredit others "is not truthful." Nor is any statement that provokes quarrels, division or resignation, he said. The truth, in the pope's reading, leads to dialogue and "fruitful results."

To achieve a climate of open-minded dialogue, Francis exalted journalists, who have been generally demonized by President Trump and other leaders in efforts to undercut critical coverage. The pope called them the "protectors of news" and characterized their profession as a "mission."

"Informing others means forming others; it means being in touch with people's lives," he wrote. "That is why ensuring the accuracy of sources and protecting communication are real means of promoting goodness, generating trust, and opening the way to communion and peace."

That message — and his appeal to cover the powerless, voiceless and downtrodden — could be found in many a Journalism 101 class. Less so his distaste for the "mad rush for a scoop" and focus on "audience impact" and "breaking news."

Also, the value on revelations that the pope seems to think is overemphasized is what many journalists would argue is the greatest service the profession can provide to the powerless, as in the case of Vatican sex abuse and financial scandals.

As the pope sees it, journalists less focused on scoops, news consumers more open to other views, and social media companies and officials more committed to safeguarding the web would open eyes to mimicry — what Francis called "that sly and dangerous form of seduction that worms its way into the heart with false and alluring arguments" — and thus cast that original and slithering bearer of fake news from the garden.

The Betoota Advocate, a Fake News Site Australians Really Love

BY ISABELLA KWAI | DEC. 26, 2017

SYDNEY, AUSTRALIA — The theme was fake news, and the crowd of young Australians at a pub in Sydney was eager to hear more. At the front of the room, two of Australia's most popular (fake) reporters grilled a panel of (real) journalists from some of the country's most established news outlets.

The fake reporters, known by their pen names Clancy Overell and Errol Parker, called a popular right-leaning newspaper "one of the last great bastions of news satire." A progressive journalist on the panel, they joked, probably owned 18 Guy Fawkes masks, associated with anarchists.

Why couldn't Australia's news media, Mr. Overell and Mr. Parker asked in October, be more like The Betoota Advocate, the small independent newspaper that they run to great success?

It was a joke that the crowd, and a growing audience of Australians, was in on. Australia's "oldest and favorite newspaper," The Betoota Advocate is increasingly one of its most widely read. It is also completely made up.

Some of the site's recent headlines include: Weekend Ruined By Adult Responsibilities, Harvey Weinstein and Bill Cosby Also Come Out As Gay and Australia Enjoys Another Peaceful Day Under Oppressive Gun Control Regime.

For three years Mr. Overell and Mr. Parker have remained steadfastly in character as proprietors of a rural newspaper. Often compared to the satirical news site The Onion, The Betoota Advocate has become the sardonic voice of disenchanted millennial Australians.

"Everyone is extremely jealous of Betoota because they get to write funny stuff and everyone clicks on their stuff," said Osman Faruqi, a panelist at the pub and an editor at Junkee, a pop culture website.

But as The Betoota Advocate, which receives more than a million page views a month, has become increasingly popular, it has also risked losing its outsider status.

This year, Mr. Overell and Mr. Parker, wearing their signature Akubra bush hats, met Prime Minister Malcolm Turnbull and had a beer. That beer, Betoota Bitter, is just one of their lucrative side projects trading on the Betoota name. They also own a clothing line, Betoota Outfitters, and produce advertising content for companies like Virgin Australia. The prime minister even appeared at an event at which the pair promoted their most recent venture, "Betoota's Australia," a book about contemporary Australia.

The site's founders are tight-lipped about just how profitable their business has become, but said it became their primary source of income three months after bringing it online. Their Facebook page has close to 500,000 members, a majority of whom are between the ages of 18 and 30, a coveted advertising demographic.

To their fans' delight, Mr. Overell and Mr. Parker insist on staying in character for public appearances and refuse to acknowledge that their journalism is really just comedy.

"We'd just like to point out we're independent regional news; we don't go by the term satire, Mr. Prime Minister." Mr. Overell told the country's leader in October.

On one hand The Betoota Advocate purports to be written in the voice of the rural working class, or what the men call "conservative." But Mr. Overell and Mr. Parker concede that their real mission is to make content that is inclusive and accessible to all sorts of people from all across Australia. In the past, they said, journalism was an exclusive club, limited to graduates from the country's elite universities.

While Australia's spiritual heart is in the Outback, more than 70 percent of the population lives in cities. If urban elites are the butt of many of the site's jokes, they do not seem to mind.

"The comedy is very disarming," said Liam Brown, 19, a student at the University of New South Wales who attended the pub panel. "They get to the heart of the issue surprisingly effectively."

Brazil Looks to Crack Down on Fake News Ahead of Bitter Election

BY ERNESTO LONDOÑO | FEB. 17, 2018

RIO DE JANEIRO — Worried that Brazilians will soon be flooded with fake news ahead of a critical presidential election, the country is setting out to crack down on organized efforts to intentionally mislead voters.

The officials leading the effort argue that the right to free speech cannot come at the expense of an illegitimate outcome, in an election that could dramatically alter the course of Brazil, the world's fourth-largest democracy.

"It is necessary to consider which of these two principles must be sacrificed in the name of an election that is neutral and not tainted by deceitful news," said Luiz Fux, a Supreme Court justice who recently assumed the presidency of the Supreme Electoral Tribunal, the highest authority on election laws and regulations. "Sometimes the excessive concern with freedom of expression ends up violating a more important principle — the democratic principle."

At Justice Fux's direction, Brazil's Federal Police recently established a task force of law enforcement and intelligence personnel, which is developing strategies to prevent fake news from being produced and to limit its reach once misleading content starts spreading online.

"It is not our intention to infringe on anyone's freedom of expression or their right to voice an opinion," said Eugênio Ricas, the director of the Federal Police's organized crime division, who is leading the fake news task force. "The big question is when does a personal opinion become a lie about a candidate that is published with the specific intent of harming them and in doing so interfering with an election."

Judicial officials say the task force is studying the tactics used by groups that have been active in spreading fake news in the past and assessing under which current laws they could most effectively be charged. They have also been consulting and negotiating with American technology companies, including Google, Twitter, Facebook and WhatsApp, in hopes of turning them into partners in the fight against fake news rather than targets of enforcement actions and fines.

If their initiative succeeds, Brazilian officials say that the October election, which will take place in a deeply polarized society, could serve as a template to address a problem that has undermined faith in democracy across the world.

But officials acknowledge that they are up against vexing legal, technological and ethical quandaries. Key among them is a 2014 law that gives internet users in Brazil strong privacy and freedom of expression protections.

While officials are mainly concerned about fake news strategies deployed by rival campaigns, not a foreign power, they caution that such tactics are often planned and executed abroad, which makes shutting them down difficult.

Judicial and law enforcement officials have called on Congress to pass a law establishing clear rules and penalties for fake news. A bill introduced last year in the Senate would make intentionally spreading false information about issues that affect public health, public safety, the economy and the electoral process punishable by up to two years in prison.

Yet it is unlikely that lawmakers will pass controversial legislation before the election, according to politicians and analysts.

That leaves officials having to make use of laws and regulations they view as anachronistic for a 21st-century problem.

These include electoral and defamation penal codes that were passed before the internet existed, and a dictatorship-era public security law from the 1980s that prohibited spreading rumors with the potential to generate panic or unrest.

"Those laws are not adequate to apply to the tactics of today," Mr. Ricas said. "The evolution of the internet and communication," he added, "makes it hard to be relying on laws from the '80s, the '60s, the '40s."

The legal situation has made building constructive relationships with technology companies a pinnacle of the plan.

Social media companies like Facebook initially dismissed accusations that they had been a vehicle for sophisticated disinformation campaigns in the United States in 2016. Yet as evidence has mounted, the technology giants have sought to cast themselves as proactive stakeholders in the fight against fake news.

They have a powerful incentive to cooperate because the tribunal headed by Justice Fux is in the process of finalizing guidelines for electoral advertising online. At a time when Brazilian politicians are increasingly turning to social media rather than traditional outlets to target voters, the social media platforms are positioned to make a windfall.

This reliance on social media to get the campaigns' messages out are expected to put the companies in the cross hairs of fake news disputes, and they say they are doing what they can to combat the problem.

"The elections in Brazil are a priority for us, and we have been taking a series of steps to make sure our platform gives people a voice, encourages civic engagement and helps strengthen democracy," a press officer for Facebook said in an emailed statement. "We have made several product improvements to reduce the reach of low quality content, eliminate the economic incentives behind most fake news, and prioritize content from trustworthy and informative sources."

Google, which has been sued and fined dozens of times in Brazil as part of efforts to get online content removed, has met with judicial officials to explain the advances, and limitations, of its tools to combat fake news.

"While there is always more to do, we believe the actions we are taking will help prevent the spread of blatantly misleading, low quality and downright false information," a Google press officer said in a statement.

Law enforcement officials in Brazil have expressed particular interest in WhatsApp, the messaging app owned by Facebook, which has about 120 million active users in Brazil.

While WhatsApp is in the middle of a legal battle before Brazil's top court over its encryption practices, company representatives in Brazil recently told judicial officials they would abide by what it considered reasonable court orders requesting the suspension of accounts found to be systemically spreading fake news.

While government officials and the technology companies' representatives say their discussions have been cordial and productive to date, the companies have made it clear they do not intend to become arbiters of truth.

A BBC World Service poll last year found that 92 percent of Brazilians expressed concern about being able to discern between fact and falsehood online, the highest percentage of respondents in any country surveyed. But just what constitutes fake news is up for debate.

The two front-runners in the race — former president Luiz Inácio Lula da Silva, a leftist, and Congressman Jair Bolsonaro, a right-wing provocateur — have taken aim at news outlets for critical coverage, in much the same way President Trump has criticized American news organizations.

Mr. Bolsonaro and his surrogates, for instance, labeled fake news an article in Folha de São Paulo that raised questions about how he and his family afforded their real estate holdings on public-servant salaries.

Mr. da Silva is by far the leading target of negative fake news stories in Brazil, according to an analysis by Veja, a weekly newsmagazine, which recently published a cover story about misinformation campaigns. One example was an article falsely claiming that Mr. da Silva had said he would ascend to the presidency even if it meant trampling the federal judge who convicted him of corruption and money laundering last year.

Mr. Bolsonaro is the rare Brazilian public figure who is the subject of more fake news stories that cast him in a positive light than a negative one, according to Veja's analysis. A spokesman for Mr. Bolsonaro did not respond to an emailed query about whether the campaign considers the use of fake news a legitimate electoral tactic. Mr. de Silva recently said such tactics should not be employed.

Marina Silva, a former environment minister who is running third in the polls, announced that she was recruiting an army of volunteers to discredit the type of disinformation campaigns that she said derailed her past two bids for the presidency, in 2010 and 2014. False stories spread on social media about Ms. Silva before those elections included a claim that, as an evangelical, she intended to ban video games and an accusation that her bodyguards once fatally beat a gay man who tried to approach her.

While there is widespread agreement among Brazilians that fake news has had a corrosive effect on the country's democracy, some worry about the ramifications of a government crackdown. The Internet Rights Coalition, a civil society group that opposes regulation and censorship of online content, recently issued a public letter raising alarm about Brazil's plans.

"We have already seen troublesome initiatives and a proliferation of laws aiming at active monitoring and regulating of online speech and delegating fact-checking to authorities," the group said.

But Justice Fux pointed to the American election as a cautionary tale about what can happen if there is no effort to check false information.

"In the American election, freedom of expression trumped over fake news," he said. "Here in our country we recognize that while a right may be exercised, it can also be abused."

Italy Braces for Fake News as Election Approaches

BY ILIANA MAGRA | MARCH 1, 2018

WITH EUROPE'S next major election set to take place in Italy on Sunday, fears that false information could mislead voters have again surfaced.

Misinformation has thrived on social media, where it can be difficult to tell the difference between real and false quotes, images and articles.

And with internet companies and governments struggling to keep up with the waves of false reports, politicians have expressed concern about how the misinformation might skew the voting process and stoke tensions.

Here are examples of how false information has spread in Europe recently, polarizing opinions about contentious topics like Muslim immigration.

A CZECH SMEAR CAMPAIGN

Jiri Drahos was the main opponent of President Milos Zeman in the Czech presidential election in January.

In the summer of 2017, Aeronet News, a Czech news website that has been linked to fake news in the past and that has a distinctly pro-Russia bent, published an article insinuating that Mr. Drahos had committed acts of pedophilia and that he had collaborated with the secret police in the 1980s.

After the article received lots of attention, Mr. Drahos released a statement on his website in which he denied the allegations, but the damage, it seems, had already been done.

FALSE MAPS IN FRANCE

Two months before the French presidential election of 2017, Bernard Barrier, who claimed to be a former employee of the French Ministry of Defense, posted a map that he said showed the locations of clashes between immigrants and the police.

The map was shared more than 15,600 times on Facebook. But it was later proved that the image had been taken from an article in the British newspaper The Daily Telegraph article, published in 2005, about riots mainly by mobs of young people from poor neighborhoods.

Immigration played a crucial role in the campaigning, and Marine Le Pen, of the far-right National Front, made the final round of voting. But she was beaten by the center-right politician Emmanuel Macron.

A SELFIE IS SKEWED IN GERMANY

Chancellor Angela Merkel of Germany visited refugees in Berlin in 2015. While there, Anas Modamani, a Syrian refugee, took a selfie with her, which he then posted to his Facebook account.

Then came the Brussels attacks in March 2016. When a photograph of the prime suspect was publicized, the selfie with Ms. Merkel, who had been under pressure for her open-door policy toward refugees, started circulating on social media — but with Mr. Modamani falsely identified as one of the bombers.

Mr. Modamani sued Facebook in an attempt to prevent its users from further reposting the picture, but he lost the case.

POLICE VIOLENCE IN SPAIN

On the day in October that Catalan secessionists voted for independence from Spain, a Twitter account with the name Persian Rose shared a video that claimed to show violence by the Spanish police against voters in Catalonia.

The post received more than 3,900 retweets. Even though the video featured the unsavory actions of Spanish police officers, the footage had nothing to do with the vote in Catalonia.

It was about a general strike and was first posted to YouTube in 2012.

PHOTO IS NOT ALL IT SEEMS IN BRITAIN

A few hours after a deadly terrorist attack on Westminster Bridge in London in March 2017, a post on Twitter accused a woman wearing a hijab of paying "no mind to the terror attack" and of "casually" walking by a dying man.

It was quickly shared widely on social media.

But the moment described in the photograph was misrepresented and out of context. Twitter later identified the account, which at the time went by the description "proud Texan and American patriot," as Russia-based.

Fears also persist that Russian interference played a role in Britain's vote in 2016 to leave the European Union.

Europe Combats a New Foe of Political Stability: Fake News

BY MARK SCOTT AND MELISSA EDDY | FEB. 20, 2017

BRUSSELS — They scan websites and pore over social media, combing through hundreds of reports a day. But the bogus claims just keep coming.

Germans are fleeing their country, fearful of Muslim refugees. The Swedish government supports the Islamic State. The European Union has drafted rules to regulate the ethnicity of snowmen.

In their open-plan office overlooking a major thoroughfare in Brussels, an 11-person team known as East Stratcom, serves as Europe's front line against this onslaught of fake news.

Created by the European Union to address "Russia's ongoing disinformation campaigns," the team — composed of diplomats, bureaucrats and former journalists — tracks down reports to determine whether they are fake. Then, it debunks the stories for hapless readers. In the 16 months since the team has been on the job, it has discredited 2,500 stories, many with links to Russia.

In a year when the French, Germans and Dutch will elect leaders, the European authorities are scrambling to counter a rising tide of fake news and anti-European Union propaganda aimed at destabilizing people's trust in institutions.

As officials play catch-up in the fight against sophisticated hacking and fake news operations, they fear Europe and its elections remain vulnerable at a critical moment: The region's decades-old project of unity hangs in the balance, challenged by populist forces within the bloc and pressures from Russia and beyond.

"If you look at how European media, and even big American media, are covering the issue now, I would say that it is those few people on that team who have been able to raise awareness," said Jakub Janda, a deputy director with European Values, a think tank based in Prague, who has worked with East Stratcom.

Many false claims target politicians who present the biggest obstacles to Moscow's goal of undermining the European Union. Others seek to portray refugees from the Middle East as terrorists or rapists, fomenting populist anger.

In France, the head of the En Marche! party said last week that Russian news channels had targeted the presidential candidate Emmanuel Macron, who belongs to the party and is running on a pro-European Union platform. Richard Ferrand, the party's secretary-general, said the campaign's databases and websites had been hit by "hundreds, if not thousands," of attacks from inside Russia.

The East Stratcom team is the first to admit that it is outgunned: The task is overwhelming, the volume of reports immense, the support to combat them scant.

The team tries to debunk bogus items in real time on Facebook and Twitter and publishes daily reports and a weekly newsletter on fake stories to its more than 12,000 followers on social media.

But its list of 2,500 fake reports is small compared with the daily churn across social media. Catching every fake news story would be nearly impossible, and the fake reports the team does combat routinely get a lot more viewers than its myth-busting efforts.

East Stratcom is purely a communications exercise. Still, team members, most of whom speak Russian, have received death threats, and a Czech member of the team has twice been accused on Russian television of espionage.

The team in Brussels is not the only force in Europe fighting the problem. Similar groups are being created from Finland to the Czech Republic to disprove online hoaxes, state agencies are improving online security to counter potential hacking attacks and European news media outlets are expanding fact-checking teams to counter false reports.

One of the biggest problems policy makers across Europe say they face is a lack of tech specialists. Germany recently passed a cybersecurity law that called for a rapid response team to combat hacking attacks. Officials quietly acknowledged, though, that they would need three teams, if they could only find people to staff them.

"There are concerns shared by many governments that fake news could become weaponized," said Damian Collins, a British politician in charge of a new parliamentary investigation examining the phenomenon. "The spread of this type of material could eventually undermine our democratic institutions."

Despite the regionwide push to counter false reports, experts question whether such fact-checking efforts by governments and publishers will have a meaningful effect. Fake reports can easily be shared through social media with few, if any, checks for accuracy.

"Most people just don't care about where their news comes from," said Mark Deuze, a professor at the University of Amsterdam. He added that "nep news," Dutch for "fake news," has been growing ahead of the country's national elections next month. "People are exposed to a ridiculous amount of information online."

Officials are also anxious about hackers' attempts to infiltrate the email accounts of candidates and politicians to steal compromising information.

Much like their American counterparts, security experts warn, European politicians remain highly vulnerable, though national intelligence agencies are now strengthening lawmakers' security protocols.

In Germany, where Chancellor Angela Merkel is facing tough competition ahead of elections in September, the country's domestic intelligence service already has reported a sharp rise in so-called phishing attacks in recent months aimed at political parties and members of the country's Parliament.

They attribute these efforts to the hacking group known as Fancy Bear, or APT 28, which American intelligence agencies linked to the hacking of the Democratic National Committee before the presidential election. Both American and German intelligence officials believe the group is operated by the G.R.U., the Russian military intelligence service.

The German government is weighing potential hefty fines for tech giants like Google and Facebook, whose platforms allow false stories to be quickly circulated. The companies insist that they cannot be held responsible because they do not generate the stories.

Hans-Georg Maassen, the head of Germany's domestic intelligence service, said that although there was no "smoking gun," Russia was likely to be involved in the increase in online misinformation aimed at destabilizing German politics.

"What makes cyberattacks so sexy for foreign powers is that it is nearly impossible to find a smoking gun," Mr. Maassen said in an interview with Phoenix TV Feb. 12. "It is always possible to cover your tracks and operate undercover."

American tech giants also have stepped in after they were accused of not doing enough to counter false reports on their platforms, accusations that Facebook, Google and other companies deny. They are now funding initiatives in the United States, France and elsewhere to flag fake news online and remove posts if they are found to violate companies' terms of use or local laws.

"This isn't just about debunking falsehoods," said Jenni Sargent, the managing director of First Draft News, a nonprofit that is partly funded by Google and expanding rapidly in France ahead of the country's elections, as well as across Europe and beyond. "What we're trying to do is to deal with the content as opposed to the source."

Such efforts across Europe have gained momentum since the United States' presidential election.

Soon after Donald J. Trump's victory in November, David Alandete gathered his team in the El País newsroom in downtown Madrid with one goal in mind: to respond to fake news.

Like many journalists, Mr. Alandete, the Spanish newspaper's managing editor and a former United States correspondent, had seen waves of false reports during the presidential campaign, many directed at Mexico — a country that accounts for roughly half of El País' online readership.

"Trump winning was a major turning point for us," Mr. Alandete said. "Many of our readers were asking whether they could even travel to the States."

Populist parties and distrust of traditional news media outlets have been growing in Spain, like other cash-strapped European countries. Such movements have spurred an explosion of fake or misleading news, aimed at either promoting certain political views or undermining others' credibility.

To counter such reports — and, in part, to cater to its Mexican readers — El País began expanding its fact-checking efforts late last year. That includes assigning five more reporters to debunk false reports online and starting a blog, called "Hechos," or "facts" in Spanish, to dispel the worst offenders.

Not all of El País's myth-busting targets, though, have been about politics.

In its first blog post, published last month, the newspaper's reporters reviewed false claims that the Portuguese soccer star Cristiano Ronaldo had abandoned his sports car after hurting one of his hands while driving. The post, according to Mr. Alandete, was viewed more than 200,000 times — making it one of El País's most-read online articles that week.

"Many people don't trust institutions anymore," Mr. Alandete said. "We see fake news coming from everywhere."

Glossary

colloquial Common, informal language.

fact-checker A person who works to verify claims made publicly or in print.

hacker Computer expert, often (but not always) associated with those who break into secure systems for illegal or malicious reasons.

hoax Deception, perhaps as a joke.

incentive Reasons for a particular action; a reward.

inflame Make a situation worse or more intense.

litigate Take a claim to court; more generally, to carefully judge a claim using evidence and reason.

objective A state of affairs in the world, not based on how people perceive it or what opinions they have about it.

partisan A strong supporter of a political movement or idea; prejudiced toward a political idea.

polarize To separate groups into extreme opposites or distinct and competitive tribes, teams, or communities.

proliferation Expansion or growth in number.

refute To prove an argument false, to counter an argument using evidence.

remunerate To pay someone for work.

rigged Designed to unfairly favor a particular outcome.

satire Humor or irony that is meant to criticize.

skepticism Doubt that something is true or real; withholding judgment until new evidence appears.

subjective Judgments based on opinion, personal point of view, or culturally relative ideas.

torrent A sudden influx or outpouring of something (as in, a torrent of emotions or complaints).

traffic Concerning websites, the number of people who visit a site or read an online article.

voracious Having a large appetite for something; insatiable.

Media Literacy Terms

"Media literacy" refers to the ability to access, understand, critically assess, and create media. The following terms are important components of media literacy, and they will help you critically engage with the articles in this title.

angle The aspect of a news story that a journalist focuses on and develops.

attribution The method by which a source is identified or by which facts and information are assigned to the person who provided them.

balance Principle of journalism that both perspectives of an argument should be presented in a fair way.

bias A disposition of prejudice in favor of a certain idea, person, or perspective.

byline Name of the writer, usually placed between the headline and the story.

caption Identifying copy for a picture; also called a legend or cutline.

chronological order Method of writing a story presenting the details of the story in the order in which they occurred.

column Type of story that is a regular feature, often on a recurring topic, written by the same journalist, generally known as a columnist.

commentary Type of story that is an expression of opinion on recent events by a journalist generally known as a commentator.

credibility The quality of being trustworthy and believable, said of a journalistic source.

critical review Type of story that describes an event or work of art, such as a theater performance, film, concert, book, restaurant, radio or television program, exhibition, or musical piece, and offers critical assessment of its quality and reception.

editorial Article of opinion or interpretation.

fake news A fictional or made-up story presented in the style of a legitimate news story, intended to deceive readers; also commonly used as an insult to criticize legitimate news that one dislikes because of its perspective or unfavorable coverage of a subject.

feature story Article designed to entertain as well as to inform.

headline Type, usually 18 point or larger, used to introduce a story.

human interest story Type of story that focuses on individuals and how events or issues affect their lives, generally offering a sense of relatability to the reader.

impartiality Principle of journalism that a story should not reflect a journalist's bias and should contain balance.

intention The motive or reason behind something, such as the publication of a news story.

interview story Type of story in which the facts are gathered primarily by interviewing another person or persons.

inverted pyramid Method of writing a story using facts in order of importance, beginning with a lead and then gradually adding paragraphs in order of relevance from most interesting to least interesting.

motive The reason behind something, such as the publication of a news story or a source's perspective on an issue.

news story An article or style of expository writing that reports news, generally in a straightforward fashion and without editorial comment.

op-ed An opinion piece that reflects a prominent journalist's opinion on a topic of interest.

paraphrase The summary of an individual's words, with attribution, rather than a direct quotation of their exact words.

plagiarism An attempt to pass another person's work as one's own without attribution.

quotation The use of an individual's exact words indicated by the use of quotation marks and proper attribution.

reliability The quality of being dependable and accurate, said of a journalistic source.

rhetorical device Technique in writing intending to persuade the reader or communicate a message from a certain perspective.

source The origin of the information reported in journalism.

sports reporting Type of story that reports on sporting events or topics related to sports.

style A distinctive use of language in writing or speech; also a news or publishing organization's rules for consistent use of language with regards to spelling, punctuation, typography, and capitalization, usually regimented by a house style guide.

tone A manner of expression in writing or speech.

Media Literacy Questions

1. Identify the various sources cited in the article "For Pope Francis, Fake News Goes Back to the Garden of Eden" (on page 186). How does the journalist attribute information to each of these sources in their article? How effective are their attributions in helping the reader identify their sources?

2. What is the intention of the article "'Fake News,' Trump's Obsession, Is Now a Cudgel for Strongmen" (on page 175)? How effectively does it achieve its intended purpose?

3. Compare the headlines of "'Alternative Facts' and the Costs of Trump-Branded Reality" (on page 145) and "Am I Imagining This?" (on page 163). Which is a more compelling headline, and why? How could the less compelling headline be changed to draw better the reader's interest?

4. Does David Streitfeld demonstrate the journalistic principle of balance/impartiality in their article "For Fact-Checking Website Snopes, a Bigger Role Brings More Attacks" (on page 46)? If so, how did they do so? If not, what could they have included to make their article more balanced/impartial?

5. What type of story is "Fake News and Bots May Be Worrisome, but Their Political Power Is Overblown" (on page 130)? Can you identify another article in this collection that is the same type of story?

6. What type of story is "10 Times Trump Spread Fake News" (on page 132)? Can you identify another article in this collection that is the same type of story?

7. What type of story is "'Alternative Facts' and the Costs of Trump-Branded Reality" (on page 145)? Can you identify another article in this collection that is the same type of story?

8. Do Mark Scott and Melissa Eddy demonstrate the journalistic principle of balance/impartiality in their article "Europe Combats a New Foe of Political Stability: Fake News" (on page 202)? If so, how did they do so? If not, what could they have included to make their article more balanced/impartial?

9. The article "Am I Imagining This?" (on page 163) is an example of an op-ed. Identify how Roger Cohen's attitude, tone, and bias help convey their opinion on the topic.

10. What is the intention of the article "How to Fight 'Fake News' (Warning: It Isn't Easy)" (on page 30)? How effectively does it achieve its intended purpose?

11. Compare the headlines of "For Fact-Checking Website Snopes, a Bigger Role Brings More Attacks" (on page 46) and "It's True: False News Spreads Faster and Wider. And Humans Are to Blame." (on page 41). Which is a more compelling headline, and why? How could the less compelling headline be changed to draw better the reader's interest?

12. Does "Inside a Fake News Sausage Factory: 'This Is All About Income'" (on page 10) use multiple sources? What are the strengths of using multiple sources in a journalistic piece? What are the weaknesses of relying heavily on one source/few sources?

13. "How Fake News Turned a Small Town Upside Down" (on page 91) features a series of photographic portraits. What do these portraits add to the article?

14. What is the intention of the article "The Real Story About Fake News Is Partisanship" (on page 114)? How effectively does it achieve its intended purpose?

15. Identify each of the sources in "Media's Next Challenge: Overcoming the Threat of Fake News" (on page 86) as a primary source or a secondary source. Evaluate the reliability and credibility of each sources. How does your evaluation of each source change your perspective on this article?

Citations

All citations in this list are formatted according to the Modern Language Association's (MLA) style guide.

BOOK CITATION

NEW YORK TIMES EDITORIAL STAFF, THE. *Fake News: Read All About It*. New York: New York Times Educational Publishing, 2019.

ARTICLE CITATIONS

CAREY, BENEDICT. "'Fake News': Wide Reach but Little Impact, Study Suggests." *The New York Times*, 2 Jan. 2018, https://www.nytimes.com/2018/01/02/health/fake-news-conservative-liberal.html.

CAREY, BENEDICT. "How Fiction Becomes Fact on Social Media." *The New York Times*, 20 Oct. 2017, https://www.nytimes.com/2017/10/20/health/social-media-fake-news.html.

CHOKSHI, NIRAJ. "How to Fight 'Fake News' (Warning: It Isn't Easy)." *The New York Times*, 18 Sept. 2017, https://www.nytimes.com/2017/09/18/business/media/fight-fake-news.html.

COHEN, ROGER. "Am I Imagining This?" *The New York Times*, 10 Feb. 2017, https://www.nytimes.com/2017/02/10/opinion/preserving-the-sanctity-of-all-facts.html.

DAVIES, WILLIAM. "The Age of Post-Truth Politics." *The New York Times*, 24 Aug. 2016, https://www.nytimes.com/2016/08/24/opinion/campaign-stops/the-age-of-post-truth-politics.html.

DICKERSON, CAITLIN. "How Fake News Turned a Small Town Upside Down." *The New York Times*, 26 Sept. 2017, https://www.nytimes.com/2017/09/26/magazine/how-fake-news-turned-a-small-town-upside-down.html.

ERLANGER, STEVEN. "'Fake News,' Trump's Obsession, Is Now a Cudgel for Strongmen." *The New York Times*, 12 Dec. 2017, https://www.nytimes.com/2017/12/12/world/europe/trump-fake-news-dictators.html.

FANDOS, NICHOLAS. "White House Pushes 'Alternative Facts.' Here Are the Real Ones." *The New York Times*, 22 Jan. 2017, https://www.nytimes.com/2017/01/22/us/politics/president-trump-inauguration-crowd-white-house.html.

FLEGENHEIMER, MATT, AND MICHAEL M. GRYNBAUM. "Trump Hands Out 'Fake News Awards,' Sans the Red Carpet." *The New York Times*, 17 Jan. 2018, https://www.nytimes.com/2018/01/17/business/media/fake-news-awards.html.

FRENKEL, SHEERA, ET AL. "In Some Countries, Facebook's Fiddling Has Magnified Fake News." *The New York Times*, 14 Jan. 2018, https://www.nytimes.com/2018/01/14/technology/facebook-news-feed-changes.html.

FRENKEL, SHEERA, AND KATIE BENNER. "To Stir Discord in 2016, Russians Turned Most Often to Facebook." *The New York Times*, 17 Feb. 2018, https://www.nytimes.com/2018/02/17/technology/indictment-russian-tech-facebook.html.

FRENKEL, SHEERA, AND SAPNA MAHESHWARI. "Facebook to Let Users Rank Credibility of News." *The New York Times*, 19 Jan. 2018, https://www.nytimes.com/2018/01/19/technology/facebook-news-feed.html.

FRIEDMAN, VANESSA. "Fake News Jeans: Travesty or Sign of Our Era?" *The New York Times*, 10 Jan. 2018, https://www.nytimes.com/2018/01/10/fashion/topshop-fake-news-jeans-controversy.html.

HERRMAN, JOHN. "Facebook's Problem Isn't Fake News — It's the Rest of the Internet." *The New York Times*, 22 Dec. 2016, https://www.nytimes.com/2016/12/22/magazine/facebooks-problem-isnt-fake-news-its-the-rest-of-the-internet.html.

HIGGINS, ANDREW, ET AL. "Inside a Fake News Sausage Factory: 'This Is All About Income.'" *The New York Times*, 25 Nov. 2016, https://www.nytimes.com/2016/11/25/world/europe/fake-news-donald-trump-hillary-clinton-georgia.html.

HOROWITZ, JASON. "For Pope Francis, Fake News Goes Back to the Garden of Eden." *The New York Times*, 24 Jan. 2018, https://www.nytimes.com/2018/01/24/us/politics/pope-francis-fake-news.html.

ISAAC, MIKE. "Facebook Mounts Effort to Limit Tide of Fake News." *The New York Times*, 15 Dec. 2016, https://www.nytimes.com/2016/12/15/technology/facebook-fake-news.html.

KWAI, ISABELLA. "The Betoota Advocate, a Fake News Site Australians Really Love." *The New York Times*, 26 Dec. 2017, https://www.nytimes.com/2017/

12/26/world/australia/betoota-advocate-fake-news.html.

LOHR, STEVE. "It's True: False News Spreads Faster and Wider. And Humans Are to Blame." *The New York Times*, 8 Mar. 2018, https://www.nytimes.com/2018/03/08/technology/twitter-fake-news-research.html.

LONDOÑO, ERNESTO. "Brazil Looks to Crack Down on Fake News Ahead of Bitter Election." *The New York Times*, 17 Feb. 2018, https://www.nytimes.com/2018/02/17/world/americas/brazil-election-fake-news.html.

MAGRA, ILIANA. "Italy Braces for Fake News as Election Approaches." *The New York Times*, 1 Mar. 2018, https://www.nytimes.com/2018/03/01/world/europe/fake-news-italy-election-europe.html.

MAHESHWARI, SAPNA. "10 Times Trump Spread Fake News." *The New York Times*, 18 Jan. 2017, https://www.nytimes.com/interactive/2017/business/media/trump-fake-news.html.

THE NEW YORK TIMES . "Facebook and the Digital Virus Called Fake News." *The New York Times*, 19 Nov. 2016, https://www.nytimes.com/2016/11/20/opinion/sunday/facebook-and-the-digital-virus-called-fake-news.html.

NYHAN, BRENDAN. "Fake News and Bots May Be Worrisome, but Their Political Power Is Overblown." *The New York Times*, 13 Feb. 2018, https://www.nytimes.com/2018/02/13/upshot/fake-news-and-bots-may-be-worrisome-but-their-political-power-is-overblown.html.

OSGOOD, KENNETH. "The C.I.A.'s Fake News Campaign." *The New York Times*, 13 Oct. 2017, https://www.nytimes.com/2017/10/13/opinion/cia-fake-news-russia.html.

PETERS, JEREMY W. "Wielding Claims of 'Fake News,' Conservatives Take Aim at Mainstream Media." *The New York Times*, 25 Dec. 2016, https://www.nytimes.com/2016/12/25/us/politics/fake-news-claims-conservatives-mainstream-media-.html.

ROOSE, KEVIN. "Here Come the Fake Videos, Too." *The New York Times*, 4 Mar. 2018, https://www.nytimes.com/2018/03/04/technology/fake-videos-deepfakes.html.

RUTENBERG, JIM. " 'Alternative Facts' and the Costs of Trump-Branded Reality." *The New York Times*, 22 Jan. 2017, https://www.nytimes.com/2017/01/22/business/media/alternative-facts-trump-brand.html.

RUTENBERG, JIM. "Media's Next Challenge: Overcoming the Threat of Fake News." *The New York Times*, 6 Nov. 2016, https://www.nytimes.com/2016/11/07/business/media/medias-next-challenge-overcoming-the-threat-of-fake-news.html.

SCOTT, MARK, AND MELISSA EDDY. "Europe Combats a New Foe of Political Stability: Fake News." *The New York Times*, 20 Feb. 2017, https://www.nytimes.com/2017/02/20/world/europe/europe-combats-a-new-foe-of-political-stability-fake-news.html.

SHANE, SCOTT. "From Headline to Photograph, a Fake News Masterpiece." *The New York Times*, 18 Jan. 2017. NYTimes.com, https://www.nytimes.com/2017/01/18/us/fake-news-hillary-clinton-cameron-harris.html.

STEPHENS, BRET. "The President Versus 'Fake News,' Again." *The New York Times*, 29 June 2017. NYTimes.com, https://www.nytimes.com/2017/06/29/opinion/trump-cnn-fake-news-russia.html.

STREITFELD, DAVID. "For Fact-Checking Website Snopes, a Bigger Role Brings More Attacks." *The New York Times*, 25 Dec. 2016. NYTimes.com, https://www.nytimes.com/2016/12/25/technology/for-fact-checking-website-snopes-a-bigger-role-brings-more-attacks.html.

TAUB, AMANDA. " 'Kompromat' and the Danger of Doubt and Confusion in a Democracy." *The New York Times*, 15 Jan. 2017. NYTimes.com, https://www.nytimes.com/2017/01/15/world/europe/kompromat-donald-trump-russia-democracy.html.

TAUB, AMANDA. "The Real Story About Fake News Is Partisanship." *The New York Times*, 11 Jan. 2017. NYTimes.com, https://www.nytimes.com/2017/01/11/upshot/the-real-story-about-fake-news-is-partisanship.html.

TAVERNISE, SABRINA. "As Fake News Spreads Lies, More Readers Shrug at the Truth." *The New York Times*, 6 Dec. 2016. NYTimes.com, https://www.nytimes.com/2016/12/06/us/fake-news-partisan-republican-democrat.html.

WARREN, ROSSALYN. "Facebook Is Ignoring Anti-Abortion Fake News." *The New York Times*, 10 Nov. 2017. NYTimes.com, https://www.nytimes.com/2017/11/10/opinion/facebook-fake-news-abortion.html.

WILLIAMS, ALEX. "2004: When Fake News Was Cool." *The New York Times*, 9 Feb. 2018. NYTimes.com, https://www.nytimes.com/2018/02/09/style/2004-when-fake-news-was-cool.html.

WILLIAMSON, ELIZABETH. "Fake News Brings a Gunman to Washington." *The New York Times*, 5 Dec. 2016. NYTimes.com, https://www.nytimes.com/2016/12/05/opinion/fake-news-brings-a-gunman-to-washington.html.

Index